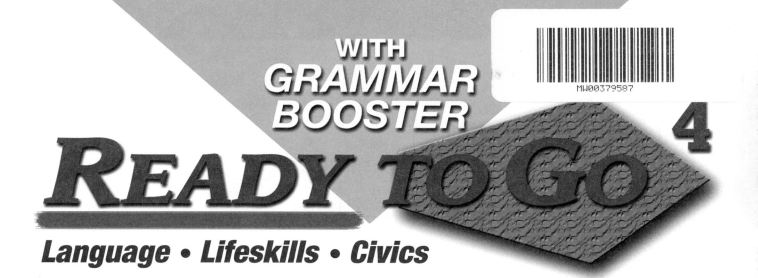

WITH GRAMMAR BOOSTER

READY TO GO 4

Language • Lifeskills • Civics

Joan Saslow

Regional Consultant Board

Ann Belletire *Illinois*	**Sandra Bergman** *New York*	**Sherie Burnette** *Texas*	**John S. Butcher** *Florida*
Michael Feher *Massachusetts*	**Susan B. Kanter** *Texas*	**Brigitte Marshall** *California*	**Monica Oliva** *Florida*

Mary E. O'Neill *Virginia*	**Grace Tanaka** *California*	**Marcia L. Taylor** *Indiana*

Edwina Hoffman
Series Advisor

Longman

Ready to Go with Grammar Booster 4: Language, Lifeskills, Civics

Pearson Education, 10 Bank Street, White Plains, NY 10606

Vice president, instructional design: Allen Ascher
Senior acquisitions editor: Marian Wassner
Senior development editor: Marcia Schonzeit
Ready to Go development editor: Julie Rouse
Vice president, director of design and production: Rhea Banker
Executive managing editor: Linda Moser
Senior production editor: Christine Lauricella
Ready to Go production editor: Marc Oliver
Production manager: Liza Pleva
Ready to Go production manager: Ray Keating
Senior manufacturing manager: Patrice Fraccio
Senior manufacturing buyer: Dave Dickey
Ready to Go manufacturing buyer: Nancy Flaggman
Cover design: Ann France
Text design: Ann France
Text composition and art direction: Word and Image Design Studio Inc.
Ready to Go text composition: Lehigh Press
Illustrations: Craig Attebery: pp. 1, 8, 22, 23, 38, 50, 53, 134; Brian Hughes: pp. 17, 23, 30, 39, 42, 43, 44, 45, 51, 58, 99, 101, 107, 108, 123; NSV: pp. 11, 24, 29, 39, 50, 53, 57, 67, 70, 71, 80, 81, 85, 93, 94, 106, 109, 121, 136; Dusan Petricic: pp. 2, 16, 22, 31, 36, 72, 73, 78, 81, 100, 114; Meryl Treatner: pp. 6, 20, 34, 48, 62, 76, 90, 92, 96, 104, 113, 118; Anna Veltfort: pp. 5, 12, 17, 26, 40, 47, 54, 68, 82, 110, 124, 138; Word and Image Design: pp. 9, 15, 19, 37, 55, 75, 78, 79, 81, 93, 120, 128, 135, 137
Photography: Gilbert Duclos: pp. 2, 3, 7, 10, 16, 17, 19, 21, 25, 30, 31, 35, 36, 44, 45, 47, 49, 51, 58, 59, 63, 65, 72, 73, 74, 77, 86, 87, 91, 100, 101, 105, 114, 115, 119, 128, 129, 133, GB-14, GB-20, GB-26
Grammar Booster: Brian Hughes: p. GB-12; Paul McCusker: p. GB-23; Suzanne Mogensen: p. GB-30; Dusan Petricic: p. GB-15; Meryl Treatner: pp. GB-3, GB-5, GB-9, GB-10, GB-21, GB-27, GB-29

ISBN: 0-13-191920-2

LONGMAN ON THE **WEB**

Longman.com offers online resources for teachers and students. Access our Companion Websites, our online catalog, and our local offices around the world.

Visit us at **longman.com**.

4 5 6 7 8 9 10—WC—08

Contents

Correlations[1]

[1]Correlations are also available at **www.longman.com/correlations**.

Unit	Correlations to National Standards			Correlations to State Standards	
	SCANS Competencies	CASAS Life Skill Competencies	EFF Content Standards	Florida	Texas
6 **Supplies and services** page 71	• Acquires and evaluates information • Uses computers to access and process data	2.4.1, 3.2.3, 3.2.4	A full range of EFF Content Standards are included in this unit. The following are emphasized: • Read With Understanding 1–3 • Convey Ideas in Writing 1 • Speak So Others Can Understand 1–3 • Listen Actively 1–3 • Observe Critically 1	Student's Book: 74.03, 75.01, 75.02, 79.03, 79.04, 83.02, 83.05, 83.06, 83.10, 83.13, 83.14, 84.02, 85.03 Workbook: 75.01, 75.02, 79.03, 79.04, 83.05, 83.06, 83.08, 83.10, 83.14, 84.02, 85.03	Student's Book: 73.03, 74.03, 75.01, 75.02, 79.03, 79.04, 83.02, 83.05, 83.06, 83.10, 83.13, 83.14, 84.02, 85.03 Workbook: 73.03, 75.01, 75.02, 79.03, 79.04, 83.05, 83.06, 83.08, 83.10, 83.14, 84.02, 85.03
7 **Relation-ships** page 85	• Acquires and evaluates information • Uses computers to access and process data • Organizes and maintains information	1.6.4, 5.1.6, 5.3.3, 7.4.4	A full range of EFF Content Standards are included in this unit. The following are emphasized: • Read With Understanding 1–5 • Convey Ideas in Writing 1 • Speak So Others Can Understand 1–3 • Listen Actively 1–3	Student's Book: 77.02, 77.03, 80.01, 80.03, 80.04, 83.02, 83.03, 83.07, 83.08, 83.10, 83.11, 83.14, 85.03 Workbook: 75.02, 80.01, 80.04, 83.03, 83.05, 83.06, 83.08, 83.10, 83.12, 83.14, 85.03	Student's Book: 73.03, 77.02, 77.03, 80.01, 80.03, 80.04, 83.02, 83.03, 83.07, 83.08, 83.10, 83.11, 83.14, 85.03 Workbook: 73.03, 75.02, 80.01, 80.04, 83.03, 83.05, 83.06, 83.08, 83.10, 83.12, 83.14, 85.03
8 **Health and safety** page 99	• Participates as a member of a team • Acquires and evaluates information • Uses computers to access and process data • Communicates ideas to justify position	2.7.2, 3.5.2, 7.2.3, 7.4.4	A full range of EFF Content Standards are included in this unit. The following are emphasized: • Read With Understanding 1–3, 5 • Convey Ideas in Writing 1 • Speak So Others Can Understand 1–3 • Listen Actively 1–3 • Observe Critically 3, 4	Student's Book: 75.01, 75.02, 75.03, 75.04, 80.01, 83.06, 83.10, 83.14, 84.01, 84.03 Workbook: 75.01, 75.03, 83.05, 83.06, 83.08, 83.10, 83.14, 84.01, 84.03, 85.03	Student's Book: 73.03, 75.01, 75.02, 75.03, 75.04, 80.01, 83.06, 83.10, 83.14, 84.01 Workbook: 73.03, 75.01, 75.03, 83.05, 83.06, 83.08, 83.10, 83.14, 84.01, 85.03
9 **Money** page 113	• Acquires and evaluates information • Uses computers to access and process data • Communicates ideas to justify position	1.3.1, 1.3.2, 1.3.3, 1.8.4, 7.1.1	A full range of EFF Content Standards are included in this unit. The following are emphasized: • Read With Understanding 1–3 • Convey Ideas in Writing 1 • Speak So Others Can Understand 1–3 • Listen Actively 1-3 • Resolve Conflict and Negotiate 1, 3, 4	Student's Book: 76.01, 76.02, 83.04, 83.06, 83.10, 83.14 Workbook: 76.01, 76.02, 83.05, 83.06, 83.08, 83.10, 83.14, 85.03	Student's Book: 73.03, 76.01, 76.02, 83.04, 83.06, 83.10, 83.14 Workbook: 73.03, 76.01, 76.02, 83.05, 83.06, 83.08, 83.10, 83.14, 85.03
10 **Your career** page 127	• Communicates ideas to justify position • Evaluates and communicates information • Understands systems	0.1.2, 4.1.2, 7.1.1	A full range of EFF Content Standards are included in this unit. The following are emphasized: • Read With Understanding 1–3 • Convey Ideas in Writing 1 • Speak So Others Can Understand 1–3 • Listen Actively 1–3 • Cooperate With Others 1–3	Student's Book: 69.01, 69.02, 69.03, 69.04, 69.05, 70.01, 70.02, 70.03, 70.04, 70.05, 71.01, 71.02, 80.01, 83.04, 83.06, 83.10, 83.14 Workbook: 69.01, 69.02, 69.03, 69.04, 69.05, 70.01, 70.02, 70.03, 70.04, 71.01, 83.04, 83.05, 83.06, 83.08, 83.10, 83.14, 84.01, 84.03, 85.03	Student's Book: 69.01, 69.02, 69.03, 69.04, 69.05, 70.01, 70.02, 70.03, 70.04, 70.05, 71.01, 71.02, 73.03, 80.01, 83.04, 83.06, 83.10, 83.14 Workbook: 69.01, 69.02, 69.03, 69.04, 69.05, 70.01, 70.02, 70.03, 70.04, 71.01, 73.03, 83.04, 83.05, 83.06, 83.08, 83.10, 83.14, 84.01, 85.03

Scope and sequence

Unit	Lifeskills	Grammar	Grammar Booster	Social Language
1 **Your life** page 1 Grammar Booster page GB-1	• Agree to a task • Give a legitimate excuse if unable • Avoid telemarketing fraud • Decline an offer • Learn about volunteerism in the community	• The simple present tense with habitual actions, unchanging facts, and adverbs of frequency • The present continuous for actions in progress • Non-action verbs	• The simple present tense and the present continuous	How to • agree to contribute to a good cause • decline a telemarketer's solicitation
2 **The community** page 15 Grammar Booster page GB-4	• Describe a housing emergency • Understand a checklist for apartment hunters • Understand tenant rights and needs • Negotiate time	• The present perfect • The present perfect vs. the simple present tense • The present perfect with <u>for</u> or <u>since</u>	• The present perfect: <u>already</u>, <u>yet</u>, <u>still</u>, <u>ever</u>, and <u>never</u> • The present perfect review: <u>for</u> and <u>since</u>	How to • request emergency repairs • describe outages
3 **Technology** page 29 Grammar Booster page GB-7	• Keep cool under pressure • Understand traffic violations • Drive safely • Avoid road rage	• Gerunds and their functions • Infinitives of purpose	• Using gerunds • Infinitives of purpose • Verbs followed by infinitives (review)	How to • respond appropriately to a police officer • express regret related to traffic violations • describe an accident
4 **The consumer world** page 43 Grammar Booster page GB-11	• Make hotel reservations • Check in at a hotel • Evaluate travel offers • Express requests and complaints politely	• <u>Some</u> and <u>any</u> with an indefinite amount or number	• <u>Some</u> and <u>any</u>	How to • request hotel amenities • respond to a request or complaint • complain about service
5 **Time** page 57 Grammar Booster page GB-13	• Manage time • Prioritize activities • Plan to meet deadlines • Understand consequences of missing deadlines	• <u>If</u> in conditional sentences for both real and unreal conditions • Verb forms in conditional sentences • Order of clauses in conditional sentences	• Conditional sentences • Conditional questions • Order of clauses in conditional sentences	How to • express dismay • offer advice • apologize for missing an appointment

Vocabulary	Civics/Culture Concepts	Math Concepts and Practical Math Skills	Critical Thinking Skills
• Ways to volunteer • Ways to decline an offer	• Community volunteerism is a cultural tradition. • It's OK to decline a telemarketer's call.	• Understand making a cash contribution or writing a check to contribute to a good cause • Understand that charitable contributions are deductible from income taxes	• Decides how to respond to a telemarketer • Compares and contrasts volunteering in U.S.A. and home country
• Household emergencies • Utilities • Fair housing and equal opportunity terms	• Rights and responsibilities are stated in a lease. • Entitlement of renters to act on housing discrimination • The Fair Housing Act	• Understand the financial responsibilities of tenant and landlord as expressed in a lease • Use cardinal numbers in writing addresses and dates	• Determines if a landlord committed a violation • Compares and contrasts tenant rights in U.S.A. and home country
• Traffic violations • Car accidents • Reactions to car accidents • Examples of aggressive driving • Emergency equipment	• Appropriate response to a police officer in a traffic stop • Avoidance of aggressive driving • The responsibility to carry safety equipment in a car	• Understand U.S. units of measurement (miles per hour) • Use addition to calculate a score • Interpret a numerical score	• Compares and contrasts traffic and driving in U.S.A. and home country • Analyzes consequences • Evaluates safety equipment
• Hotel room amenities • Hotel services • Hotel room features	• The consumer's responsibility to evaluate travel offers • Entitlement of travelers to protect against fraud	• Understand charges on a hotel bill • Understand the advantages and disadvantages of traveler's checks, cash, credit cards, and ATM cards in traveling	• Evaluates travel offers • Makes decisions related to travel offers • Compares and contrasts tourism in U.S.A. and home country
• Consequences of missing a deadline • Appointments • Time management	• The responsibility to know deadlines for driver's license, voter registration, and childhood immunizations	• Calculate spans of time and prioritize actions based on them • Interpret a library overdue policy and calculate overdue charges	• Determines solutions to time problems • Compares and contrasts life in U.S.A. and home country • Understands consequences

Unit	Lifeskills	Grammar	Grammar Booster	Social Language
6 **Supplies and services** page 71 Grammar Booster page GB-16	• Ask for a written estimate • Make an agreement • Understand homeowner's, car, and life insurance	• Definition of a sentence • Punctuating sentences • Capitalization rules	• The sentence • Other punctuation rules	How to • ask for a written estimate • ask for and give a recommendation
7 **Relation-ships** page 85 Grammar Booster page GB-18	• Understand the elements of the U.S. justice system • State opinions respectfully	• Reporting a person's words in direct speech • Using a comma in quotations • Reporting a person's words in indirect speech	• Reporting a person's words: direct speech • Reporting a person's words: indirect speech	How to • discuss pros and cons of controversial issues • agree and disagree respectfully
8 **Health and safety** page 99 Grammar Booster page GB-21	• Avoid quackery • Separate weight-loss facts from myths • Make daily food choices based on the Food Guide Pyramid • Keep records in order to evaluate and plan	• Expressing regrets with <u>should have</u> or <u>shouldn't have</u> • Negative <u>yes</u>/<u>no</u> questions	• <u>Should have</u>/<u>shouldn't have</u> • Negative <u>yes</u>/<u>no</u> questions	How to • express regrets about food choices • suggest a remedy
9 **Money** page 113 Grammar Booster page GB-24	• Borrow money from a friend • Agree to repay a loan	• Spelling reminders • Connecting ideas with <u>but</u> and <u>so</u>	• Common misspellings • Connecting ideas with <u>and</u>, <u>but</u>, and <u>so</u>	How to • give a reason to borrow money • commit to repay a loan • share wishes and dreams • offer advice on financial aid
10 **Your career** page 127 Grammar Booster page GB-28	• Write a job history and resume • Tell someone about a hard choice	• The past unreal conditional	• The past unreal conditional	How to • tell an employer about a job offer • get a counteroffer

Vocabulary	Civics/Culture Concepts	Math Concepts and Practical Math Skills	Critical Thinking Skills
• Services the consumer should get an estimate for • Descriptions of good workers • Key insurance terms	• The importance of having insurance • The consumer's right to an estimate • It's not rude to ask for a reference.	• Compare competitive service estimates • Express dates, time, and speed in numbers	• Compares and contrasts insurance in U.S.A. and home country • Makes home-repair decisions
• Opinions pro and con • Sample pros and cons of controversial ideas • Rules • Elements of the U.S. justice system	• It's not rude to express ideas and disagree respectfully. • The U.S. Constitution and the Bill of Rights • The U.S. justice system	• Understand payment devices (cash, charge, check) and how to use them • Understand that total price is made up of sum of price and tax	• Evaluates pros and cons of controversial issues • Compares and contrasts the justice system in U.S.A. and home country
• Ways to take care of health problems • The Food Guide Pyramid	• The responsibility to understand consequences of good and bad diets • The responsibility to evaluate health claims	• Understand number of recommended servings from food groups • Consider relationship between portion and number of servings	• Evaluates diet myths and facts • Evaluates a meal plan • Compares and contrasts a healthful diet in U.S.A. and home country
• Ways to agree and decline • Reasons to borrow money from a friend • Wishes and dreams • Ways to fund dreams that are hard to afford	• Awareness of sources of financial assistance • Benefits of credit unions • Risks of payday loans and work-at-home schemes	• Compare loan options (personal loans, credit unions, bank loans, payday loans) • Understand start-up fees in work-at-home schemes • Understand finance charges on payday loans	• Evaluates work-at-home schemes • Compares and contrasts lending in U.S.A. and home country
• Some reasons to apply for a better job • Telling someone about a hard choice • Perks, benefits, and other features of good jobs	• Employees are entitled to negotiate with employers for a better job, better opportunities, and higher salary. • The responsibility to present honest job histories and resumes	• Choose jobs based on offers and counteroffers • Use chronological format to prepare a job resume	• Compares and contrasts life and work in U.S.A. and home country • Analyzes resume red flags

Acknowledgments

The author wishes to acknowledge with gratitude the following consultants and reviewers—our partners in the development of *Ready to Go*.

Regional Consultant Board

The following people have participated on an ongoing basis in shaping the content and approach of *Ready to Go*:

Ann Belletire, Northern Illinois University–Business and Industry Services, Oak Brook, Illinois • **Sandra Bergman**, Instructional Facilitator, Alternative, Adult, and Continuing Education Program, New York City Board of Education • **Sherie Burnette**, Assistant Dean, Workforce Education, Brookhaven College of the Dallas County Community College District, Farmers Branch, Texas • **Dr. John S. Butcher**, Florida DOE Department of Workforce Development, Adult ESOL Task Force • **Michael Feher**, Boston Chinatown Neighborhood Center, Boston, Massachusetts • **Susan B. Kanter**, Instructional Supervisor, Continuing Education and Contract Training, Houston Community College-Southwest, Houston, Texas • **Brigitte Marshall**, Consultant, Albany, California • **Monica Oliva**, Educational Specialist, Miami-Dade County Public Schools, Miami, Florida • **Mary E. O'Neill**, Coordinator of Community Education, ESL, Northern Virginia Community College—Annandale Campus, Annandale, Virginia • **Grace Tanaka**, Professor of ESL, Santa Ana College School of Continuing Education; ESL Facilitator, Centennial Education Center, Santa Ana, California • **Marcia L. Taylor**, Workplace Instructor, Joblink, Ispat-Inland Inc., East Chicago, Indiana

Reviewers

The following people shared their perspectives and made suggestions either by reviewing manuscript or participating in editorial conferences with the author and editors:

Leslie Jo Adams, Santa Ana College–Centennial Education Center, Santa Ana, California • **Sandra Anderson**, El Monte-Rosemead Adult School, El Monte, California • **Marcy Berquist**, San Diego Community College District, San Diego, California • **Robert Breitbard**, District School Board of Collier County, Naples, Florida • **Ruth Brigham**, A.C.C.E.S.S., Boston, Massachusetts • **Donna Burns**, Mt. San Antonio College, Walnut, California • **Eric Burton**, Downington Area School District, Downington, Pennsylvania • **Michael James Climo**, West Los Angeles College, Culver City, California • **Teresa Costa**, The English Center, Miami, Florida • **Robert Cote**, Miami-Dade County Public Schools, Miami, Florida • **Georgette Davis**, North Orange County Community College District, Orange County, California • **Janet Ennis**, Santa Ana College–Centennial Education Center, Santa Ana, California • **Peggy Fergus**, Northern Illinois University–Business and Industry Services, Oak Brook, Illinois • **Oliva Fernandez**, Hillsborough County Public Schools–Adult & Community Education, Tampa, Florida • **Elizabeth Fitzgerald**, Hialeah Adult & Community Center, Hialeah, Florida • **Marty Furch**, Palomar College, San Diego, California • **Eric Glicker**, North Orange County Community College District, Orange County, California • **Steve Gwynne**, San Diego Community College District, San Diego, California • **Victoria Hathaway**, DePaul University, Chicago, Illinois • **Jeffrey L. Janulis**, Richard J. Daley College, City Colleges of Chicago, Chicago, Illinois • **Mary Karamourtopoulos**, Northern Essex Community College, Haverhill, Massachusetts • **Shirley Kelly**, Brookhaven College of the Dallas County Community College District, Farmers Branch, Texas • **Marilou Kessler**, Jewish Vocational Service–Vocational English Program, Chicago, Illinois • **Henry Kim**, North Orange County Community College District, Orange County, California • **Dr. Maria H. Koonce**, Broward County Public Schools, Ft. Lauderdale, Florida • **John Kostovich**, South Texas Community College–Intensive English Program, McAllen, Texas • **Jacques LaCour**, Mt. Diablo Adult Education, Concord, California • **Beatrice Liebman**, Miami Sunset Adult Center, Miami, Florida • **Doris Lorden**, Wright College–Workforce Training Center, Chicago, Illinois • **Mike Lowman**, Coral Gables Adult Education Center, Coral Gables, Florida • **Lois Maharg**, Delaware Technical and Community College • **Vicki Moore**, El Monte-Rosemead Adult School, El Monte, California • **Deborah Nash**, School Board of Palm Beach County Schools, West Palm Beach, Florida • **Cindy Neubrech**, Mt. San Antonio College, Walnut, California • **Patricia Peabody**, Broward County Public Schools, Ft. Lauderdale, Florida • **Joe A. Perez**, Hillsborough County Public Schools, Tampa, Florida • **Diane Pinkley**, Teacher's College, Columbia University, New York, New York • **Kay Powell**, Santa Ana College–Centennial Education Center, Santa Ana, California • **Wendy Rader**, San Diego Community College District, San Diego, California • **Don Robison**, Jewish Vocational Service–Workplace Literacy, Chicago, Illinois • **Richard Sasso**, Triton College, River Grove, Illinois • **Mary Segovia**, El Monte-Rosemead Adult School, El Monte, California • **Laurie Shapero**, Miami-Dade Community College, Miami, Florida • **Sara Shapiro**, El Monte-Rosemead Adult School, El Monte, California • **Samanthia Spence**, Richland College, Dallas, Texas • **JoAnn Stehy**, North Orange County Community College District, Orange County, California • **Margaret Teske**, Mt. San Antonio College, Walnut, California • **Dung Tran**, North Orange County Community College District, Orange County, California • **Claire Valier**, School District of Palm Beach County, West Palm Beach, Florida • **Catherine M. Waterman**, Rancho Santiago Community College, Santa Ana, California • **James Wilson**, Mt. San Antonio College, Walnut, California

To the teacher

Ready to Go: Language, Lifeskills, Civics is a four-level, standards-based course in English as a second language. *Ready to Go* prepares adults for self-sufficiency in the three principal areas of their lives: the community, the home, and the workplace.

Communicative competence in English is of critical importance in achieving self-sufficiency. *Ready to Go* applies the best of current second language acquisition research to ensure immediate success, rapidly enabling learners to

- understand the spoken and written language of daily life.
- communicate orally and in writing.
- understand the culture and civic expectations of their new environment.
- master lifeskills necessary to survive and thrive in the American community and workplace.

To achieve these goals with efficiency and speed, *Ready to Go* weaves together three integrated strands: language, lifeskills, and civics*, tightly correlating the major state and federal standards with a complete language syllabus and relevant social language.

Course length
Ready to Go is designed to be used in a period of 60 to 90 classroom hours. This period can be shortened or lengthened, based on the needs of the group or the program. The Teacher's Edition gives detailed instructions for tailoring *Ready to Go* to specific settings, circumstances, and student groups.

Components
Student's Book
The *Ready to Go* Student's Book is a complete four-skills text, integrating listening, speaking, reading, and writing with life skills, math skills, civics concepts, and authentic practice in understanding native speech and real-life documents. The book contains 10 units, each one culminating in a concise review section.

The Correlations Charts on pages iv–v indicate how *Ready to Go* is correlated to the following national and state standards:
- SCANS competencies
- CASAS Life Skill Competencies
- EFF Content Standards
- Florida State Standards
- Texas State Standards

These correlations can also be downloaded at no cost from www.longman.com/correlations.

To assist in lesson planning, the Scope and Sequence chart (on pages vi–ix) clearly spells out the following elements for each unit:
- Lifeskills
- Grammar
- Grammar Booster
- Social language
- Vocabulary
- Civics/culture concepts
- Math concepts and practical math skills
- Critical thinking skills

In order to facilitate student-centered instruction, *Ready to Go* uses a variety of grouping strategies: pairs, groups, and whole class. In numerous activities, learners work with others to create a joint product. Those activities are labeled collaborative activities.

Two special features of the *Ready to Go* Student's Book are Do it yourself! and Authentic practice.

Because learners have an immediate need to use their new language outside the class, Do it yourself! provides a daily opportunity for students of diverse abilities to put new language into their own words. This affords them a chance to "try their wings" in the safe and supportive environment of the classroom.

Authentic practice activities create a "living language laboratory" within the classroom. Learners practice responding to authentic models of spoken and written English with the limited language they know. In this way, students build their confidence and skill in coping with the language of the real world.

As a supplement to the Practical grammar section in each *Ready to Go* unit, the Student's Book includes a comprehensive Grammar Booster at the back of the book. The Grammar Booster provides abundant additional practice for each grammar point taught in the Student's Book units. It also includes grammar charts so that students can review the grammar forms and "Things to remember" before they do an exercise. The Grammar Booster exercises can be done any time after the grammar has been introduced on the Practical grammar pages, either in class or as homework. For your convenience, a separate Answer Key is available.

Audiocassettes and Audio CDs
Because listening comprehension is a fundamental survival and success skill for new speakers of English, *Ready to Go* includes a comprehensive listening strand in each unit of the Student's Book.

---

* In *Ready to Go*, the term "civics" refers to concepts that introduce learners to expected social behavior in this culture, an understanding of which is essential *before* students can participate fully or truly understand their rights and responsibilities as citizens. The term does not refer to citizenship education.

In addition to listening comprehension activities, there are numerous other opportunities for learners to practice their listening skills. All exercises that appear on audio CD or audiocassette are marked with a 🎧 symbol. A transcript of each listening comprehension activity is located on its corresponding Teacher's Edition page, for easy reference. A Student's Audio CD, bound into each Student's Book, contains all the model conversations for listening and pronunciation practice outside of class.

Teacher's Edition
An interleaved Teacher's Edition provides page-by-page teaching suggestions that add value to the Student's Book. In addition to general and day-by-day teaching suggestions, each teacher's page includes optional activities, challenge activities, and language and culture/civics notes that will help teachers demystify and explain new language and culture concepts to students. Answers to all exercises and the audioscript of each listening comprehension activity are also readily found on all pages.

Workbook
In addition to the ample opportunities for reading and writing practice contained in the Student's Book, the *Ready to Go* Workbook contains further reading and writing exercises. The Workbook is valuable for homework or for in-class activities. An added feature is a test preparation activity for each unit, with CASAS-like and BEST Test-like items which ensure that learners can "bubble in" and cope with the formats of standardized language tests.

Teacher's Resource Binder
A three-ring binder contains a wealth of valuable items to enable busy teachers to customize their instruction and make the preparation of supplementary teaching aids unnecessary. The Classroom Booster Pack provided with the Binder features pair-work cards, vocabulary flash cards, grammar self-checks, photo chat cards, and extension activities for daily use. Also included in the Binder are the following additional teacher-support materials: Correlations of *Ready to Go* with state and federal standards, Student Progress Checklists, Pre- and Post-Tests and Achievement Tests, and Skills for Test Taking.

Review Transparencies
A special feature of the *Ready to Go* series is the full-page Review illustration located at the end of each unit. This open-ended activity is designed to elicit from students all the language they know—vocabulary, social language, and grammar. The picture provides a clear visual context for practice and helps students bridge the gap between language practice and authentic language use. The full-page illustrations are available as four-color transparencies to be used with an overhead projector. The Review transparencies come in a convenient, resealable

envelope, along with a Teacher's Notes booklet containing suggested activities.

Placement Test
A simple-to-administer test places students accurately within the *Ready to Go* series.

Ready to Go Companion Web site
The *Ready to Go* companion Web site (www.longman.com/readytogo) provides numerous additional resources for students and teachers. This no-cost, high-benefit feature includes opportunities for further practice of language and content from the *Ready to Go* Student's Book. For the teacher, there are optional strategies and materials that amplify the *Ready to Go* Teacher's Edition.

Student's Book unit contents
Each unit in the *Ready to Go* Student's Book uses an integrated three-step approach.

1. Practical conversations with integrated vocabulary
   Simple, memorable model conversations that are transferable to learners' own lives permit intensive practice of new vocabulary and key social language. These are followed by lively pair-work activities.

2. Practical grammar
   Essential grammatical structure practice enables learners to manipulate the vocabulary and practical conversations to express ideas of their own.

3. Authentic practice
   An entertaining picture story illustrates the authentic use of spoken target language and leads to a series of interactive comprehension tasks that help students cope with spoken language in the world outside the classroom.

   An extended listening text exposes students to authentic models of TV programs, lectures, radio shows, and other lively and informative conversational and non-conversational sources.

   A unique real-world reading enables students to understand culture and civics concepts of their new community and workplace. Then a series of authentic documents and other print features provides preparation for coping with life outside the classroom. *Ready to Go 4* contains both practical information and beginning citizenship education. A formal introduction to the U.S. Constitution, the Bill of Rights, and the U.S. justice system is intended to support students' full participation in the American community.

Review
Following each unit is a three-page, four-skill review for learners to check their progress.

Your life

 Preview

Warm up. Have you ever been interrupted at dinner by a telemarketer? What happened? What did you do?

Unit 1 objectives

- Agree to contribute to a good cause.
- Decline a telemarketer's sales solicitation.
- Understand the spirit of volunteerism.
- Avoid telemarketing fraud.

Practical conversations

A. Listen and read.

A: I'm collecting for the food pantry. Would you be willing to make a donation?

B: What did you say it was for?

A: The food pantry.

B: That's a good cause. I'd be happy to.

A: Thanks so much.

B. Pronunciation and intonation practice.

Vocabulary

Ways to volunteer

make a donation

volunteer some time

bake something for the bake sale

make a few phone calls

mail some letters

distribute some flyers

C. Pair work. Ask for help with a good cause. Use these or your own cause.

the homeless shelter	the food pantry
the scholarship fund	the hospital

A: I'm collecting for _____. Would you be willing to _____?

B: What did you say it was for?

A: _____.

B: That's a good cause. I'd be happy to.

A: _____.

🎧 **A. Listen and read.**

    A: Hello?

    B: Good evening. This is the ABC Telephone Company. We have a special offer on cell phone service this evening.

    A: Is this a sales call?

    B: Yes, it is.

    A: I'm sorry. We don't take offers over the phone.

    B: Thank you very much.

🎧 **B. Pronunciation and intonation practice.**

🎧 **Vocabulary**

Ways to decline an offer

We don't take offers over the phone.

We're having dinner right now.
We're not interested.
We already have _____.
We don't need _____.
Your own way: _____.

C. Pair work. Decline a telemarketer's offer. Use the name of a business that has called you or a business you know.

    A: Hello?

    B: _____. This is _____. We have a special offer on _____.

    A: Is this a sales call?

    B: Yes, it is.

    A: I'm sorry. _____.

    B: _____.

➤ Do it yourself!

A. List one or more charitable and sales solicitations you have received.

Charities	Sales
Flood Emergency Relief Fund	Manny's Chimney Cleaning

B. Pair work. Role-play a conversation accepting or declining a solicitation from your list.

Unit 1   3

Practical grammar

The simple present tense and the present continuous

Use the simple present tense to talk about habitual actions and unchanging facts.

Lee **volunteers** at the community center every Sunday.

The American Cancer Society **provides** funds for cancer research.

Use the simple present tense with *never, sometimes, often,* and *always*.

I always **ask** telemarketers to send their offers in writing.

Use the present continuous for actions in progress.

He's **talking** to a telemarketer right now.

Don't use *never, sometimes, often,* or *always* with the present continuous.

~~I'm never going there. I'm often going there.~~

A. Complete each sentence with the simple present tense or the present continuous.

1. Water _____ at 212°F.
   boils / is boiling

2. They always _____ on Mondays.
   are collecting / collect

3. When she _____, I never _____ the call.
   calls / is calling   answer / am answering

4. I can't talk right now because we _____ lunch.
   eat / are eating

5. I _____ sales offers over the phone.
   don't accept / am not accepting

6. _____ often _____ at the hospital?
   Are you / Do you   volunteering / volunteer

B. Complete each sentence with the simple present tense or the present continuous. Use verbs from the box.

collect	donate	ask	talk	bake

1. I usually _____donate to_____ clothes to the American Red Cross when they

   _____.

2. I can't distribute flyers this week, so I _____ something for the bake sale instead.

3. They never _____Talk to_____ to telemarketers during dinner.

4. She can't come to the phone right now. She's out. She _____Collect_____ for the soup kitchen.

Non-action verbs

Some verbs don't describe actions. Don't use the present continuous with non-action verbs:
appear, be, feel, hate, have, hear, know, like, look, love, need, remember, see, seem, smell, sound, taste, think, understand, want.

See page 145 for a more complete list of non-action verbs.

C. Complete the conversation with the simple present tense or the present continuous.

A: Hello?

B: Good evening. I _____ to reach Mrs. Belinda Malino. Is this she?
1. try / am trying

A: Well, I'm Mrs. Melinda Malino.

B: I'm sorry. How are you this evening, Mrs. Balino?

A: Fine, thanks. But we _____ dinner right now. Is this a sales call?
2. eat / are eating

B: No. I _____ anything now. I only _____ a minute
3. don't sell / am not selling   **4.** need / am needing

to tell you about a special offer for customers of Tri-State Telephone.

A: I'm sorry. We never _____ offers over the phone.
5. take / are taking

B: I _____. But I _____ you'll like what I have
6. understand / am understanding   **7.** think / am thinking

to tell you.

A: Please send your offer in writing. We'll be happy to look at it then.

B: Thank you very much.

➤ Do it yourself!

Pair work. Choose the name of a real company. Read Model 2 on page 3 again. Then continue the conversation for the two people in the picture.

A: Hello?
B: Good evening. How are you this evening?
A: Fine, thanks. . . .

Authentic practice

Volunteerism and charity

A. Read the picture story again. Complete each sentence.

1. The proceeds of the bake sale are going to the ___homeless shelter___.

2. The bake sale will be on ___Saturday___ at the ___railroad station___.

3. Volunteers can donate something to sell, make a cash contribution, or work the ___booth___.

B. Listen. Read each response out loud from the text.

C. Vocabulary. Circle the word or phrase closer in meaning to each underlined phrase.

1. They <u>showed up</u> too late to help set up the booth, so they worked it instead.
   left / arrived

2. <u>Make the check out to</u> the shelter.
   Write the check to / Throw the check away at

3. Not many homeless people <u>stopped by</u> the soup kitchen yesterday.
   came to / refused to come to

4. You can <u>pick up</u> cookies at the sale.
   buy / sell

5. When I got there, they had <u>run out of</u> everything. There was nothing left!
   sold / baked

D. Read each sentence or question. Underline your response.

1. "Would you be willing to work the booth?"

   YOU With pleasure.   **YOU** Is this a sales call?

2. "How many volunteers were at the soup kitchen?"

   YOU A million!   **YOU** Two. Tomato rice and chicken noodle.

3. "You could help run the booth."

   YOU Actually, I won't be able to.   **YOU** Better come early.

4. "Could you make a cash contribution?"

   YOU Sure. Who should I make   **YOU** Absolutely. It's a good cause.
   it out to?

E. Pair work. Take turns reading the items and responses in Exercise D.

➤ Do it yourself!

A. Write your own response. Then read each conversation out loud with a partner.

That's a good cause. Who should I make the check payable to?

YOU _____

Thanks for agreeing to volunteer at the booth. What time can you stop by to pick up the pies?

YOU _____

We've run out of baked goods. Could you please pick up some more at the supermarket?

YOU _____

B. Discussion. Has anyone ever asked you to volunteer? For what? What did you do?

Authentic practice

Avoiding telemarketing fraud

A. **Listening comprehension. Listen to the TV report. Then answer the question.**

Why do consumers complain about telemarketing? _____

_____

B. **Pair work. Compare answers with a partner.**

C. **Listen again if necessary. Then check** *True* **or** *False* **for each statement, according to the report.**

	True	False
1. Telemarketers sell products and services by phone.	☒	☐
2. Con artists are honest salespeople.	☐	☒
3. A free offer is always a fraud.	☐	☒
4. You should always hang up on telemarketers.	☐	☒

D. **Answer the questions about a sales call you have received at home.**

1. Who called? _____

2. What time was it? _____

3. What questions did the caller ask? _____

4. What did the caller want to sell? _____

5. Did you buy anything? _____

6. If you bought something, how did you pay? _____

7. Are you happy with the product or service? _____

E. True story. **Look at the answers you wrote in Exercise D. Then tell your partner or your group about the sales call you received at home.**

FYI. To file a complaint about a telemarketer with the Federal Trade Commission (FTC), download a complaint form from their Web site: www.ftc.gov

You can also write or call the FTC:

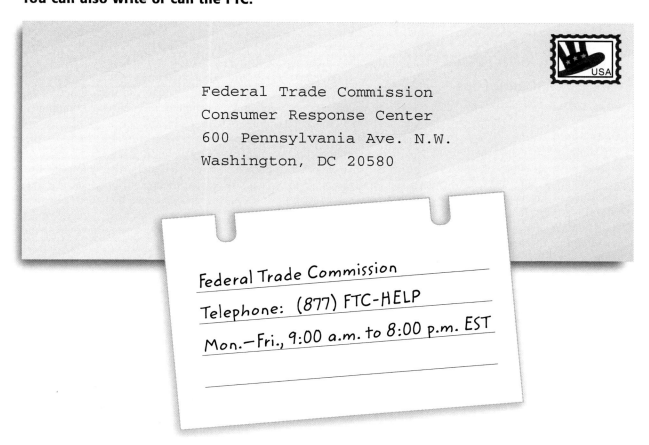

Federal Trade Commission
Consumer Response Center
600 Pennsylvania Ave. N.W.
Washington, DC 20580

USA

Federal Trade Commission

Telephone: (877) FTC-HELP

Mon.–Fri., 9:00 a.m. to 8:00 p.m. EST

➤ Do it yourself!

A. Role play. **Start with the conversation below, using your own words and ideas. Then continue until the end of the call.**
   Partner A: Answer the phone and respond to Partner B.
   Partner B: Decide whether you are a con artist or an honest salesperson.

A: _____?
B: Hello. I'm calling from _____. Are you over eighteen years old?
A: _____.
B: We have a special offer for you tonight, if you'll just answer a few questions.
A: . . .

B. Discussion. **Compare phone calls with your classmates. Was the telemarketer honest or a con artist? What did the consumer say?**

Authentic practice

Volunteerism in the local community

A. Read and listen to the letters.

Ask Joan
Culture tips for newcomers

Dear Joan:

My son is a high school junior and he wants to volunteer in the fire department of our town. He says that a lot of his friends volunteer their time too. Joan, he's still a child, and he plans to go to college, not work in a fire department. This is a job for big men, not for teenagers! He could get hurt or killed. I don't understand. Joan, what should I do?

Nero in Nashville

Dear Nero:

Congratulations on having raised a wonderful, caring son! You must be very proud of him. Your son is participating in an important tradition of our culture: volunteerism. Many people consider volunteerism a responsibility of their membership in the local and larger community.

It's not unusual for teenagers to volunteer their time at the firehouse, the ambulance corps, or the local food pantry. At the firehouse, teens under the age of eighteen usually do not fight fires, although they receive training in firefighting techniques. But they participate in the maintenance of the fire trucks and other equipment, assist firefighters at the scene of fires, and help in chores at the firehouse. Whatever your son finally chooses as a career, the time he spends volunteering to help others in need is time well spent. So, don't worry, Dad. Just be proud.

Joan

Dear Joan:

I'm a homemaker and a part-time seamstress in my own home. My two children have graduated from high school (with honors!) and both are now studying in college. Joan, they both received scholarships. I am very grateful.

Now that my children are not at home, I have some extra time and I would like to volunteer. What do you recommend?

Grateful Grace

Dear Grace:

If you belong to a church, a synagogue, or a mosque, you will find opportunities there to volunteer in your local community in a variety of activities. Non-religious institutions such as the Boy and Girl Scouts, the League of Women Voters, the volunteer fire department and ambulance corps, soup kitchens, homeless shelters, and the local food pantry would also all be happy to have you as a volunteer. Many institutions accept donated goods and financial contributions in addition to your time. And remember, you may deduct charitable contributions from your income taxes.

The following quotation from a U.S. Government Web site on volunteerism expresses a core tradition of our culture: "The generous spirit of the American people has fostered a great and long-standing tradition of service." Your volunteerism expresses that spirit!

Joan

B. Check *True, False,* or *? (No information)* for each statement.

	True	False	?
1. Nero is a volunteer firefighter.	☐	☒	☐
2. Nero's son is in high school now.	☒	☐	☐
3. Nero thinks his son's volunteer work is dangerous.	☒	☐	☐
4. Now that her children are in college, Grace is not so busy.	☒	☐	☐
5. Grace belongs to a church, synagogue, or mosque.	☐	☐	☒

10 Unit 1

C. **Discussion. Answer the questions. Then discuss with your classmates.**

1. Why is Nero in Nashville worried? _____

2. Is Joan worried too? _____

3. What do teen volunteers usually do at the firehouse? _____

_____

4. What is a volunteer? _____

FYI. Read this information about volunteering from the Web site of the U.S. Department of Housing and Urban Development (HUD).

```
┌─────────────────────────────── Volunteer Programs ──────────────────────────────┐
│ Address: @ http://www.hud.gov                                              › go  │
│                                                                                  │
│                              Volunteerism                                        │
│   Healthy communities depend on volunteers — like you! Maybe one of these        │
│   programs fits your interests.                                                  │
│                                                                                  │
│   Federal volunteer programs            National volunteer programs              │
│   • America Reads Challenge             • American Cancer Society                 │
│   • America's Outdoors Volunteers       • American Red Cross                      │
│   • AmeriCorps                          • Big Brothers, Big Sisters of America    │
│                                         • Habitat for Humanity                    │
│                                                                                  │
│   For a complete list of agencies that offer opportunities to volunteer in the   │
│   United States, click on                                                        │
│   http://www.hud.gov/volunteering/index.cfm                                      │
│   Or write to:                                                                   │
│   U.S. Department of Housing and Urban Development                               │
│   451 7th Street S.W., Washington, DC 20410                                      │
│   Telephone: (202) 708-1112, TTY: (202) 708-1455                                 │
│   For information about volunteering in Canada, click on                         │
│   http://www.nsgvp.org/n-f2-ca.htm                                               │
│                                                                                  │
│  Web zone                                                                        │
└──────────────────────────────────────────────────────────────────────────────────┘
```

➤ Do it yourself!

A. **In your home country, how do people help others? Fill in the chart.**

Country	Donations or contributions	Volunteer opportunities
U.S.	United Way	soup kitchen at shelter

B. **Culture talk. In the country you come from, is there a tradition of service to the community? How do people help each other? Do they collect money? Do they volunteer? Compare cultures with your classmates.**

> # Review
>
> ## A. Pair work or group work.
>
> - Who are the people?
> - What are they doing?
>
> Ask and answer questions.
>
> Create conversations.
>
> Tell a story.
>
> Say as much as you can.

⌒ B. Listening comprehension. Listen to the conversation. Then listen again and check *True* or *False* for each statement.

		True	False
1.	The man says the family is eating.	❑	❑
2.	The man wants to talk to the caller.	❑	❑
3.	The caller is a telemarketer.	❑	❑
4.	The caller isn't selling anything.	❑	❑
5.	*Parent and Child* is the name of a magazine.	❑	❑
6.	You can buy *Parent and Child* on the newsstand.	❑	❑
7.	The caller is sending something in writing on Tuesday.	❑	❑
8.	The man accepts the offer.	❑	❑

C. Complete the conversation with the simple present tense or the present continuous.

A: Hey, Mark. I _____ that car!
                    1. love / am loving

B: Thanks! What _____ in this neighborhood?
                 2. do you do / are you doing

A: I _____ used furniture for the refugee housing project.
         3. pick up / am picking up

    I _____ to set up a house for a new family this week.
         4. try / am trying

B: That's a good cause. Refugees _____ absolutely nothing when
                        5. have / are having

    they _____ here.
        6. get / are getting

A: That's true. By the way, would you be willing to make a few phone calls for us?

    We really _____ help.
           7. need / are needing

B: How much time _____?
               8. do you need / are you needing

A: About two million hours! No, seriously, if you _____ a few
                                       9. have / are having
    hours any evening this week, that would be great.

B: I _____. Well, I _____ I can make it on Thursday.
      10. understand / am understanding   **11.** think / am thinking

D. Read each sentence or question. Underline your response.

1. "I'm collecting groceries for the women's shelter. Would you be willing to make a donation?"

   (YOU) Yes. Please drop it off at 4:00.   (YOU) Yes. What do you need?

2. "What did you say you were collecting for?"

   (YOU) The scholarship fund.   (YOU) I never take sales calls.

3. "Could you pick up some flyers to distribute this afternoon?"

   (YOU) Sure. I'll stop by after work.   (YOU) There you go!

4. "I ran out of checks."

   (YOU) You could make a cash contribution.   (YOU) We're not interested.

5. "We're running a clothing drive for the state hospital."

   (YOU) That's great. I can volunteer some time.   (YOU) Did you run out yet?

E. Choose a word or phrase for each definition. Fill in the ovals.

1. selling goods and services over the phone

   (a) telemarketing   (b) fraud

2. a dishonest person who lies to get a consumer's money

   (a) a con artist   (b) a telemarketer

3. a dishonest offer, in which a person tries to steal money from a consumer

   (a) a telephone sales call   (b) fraud

4. a person who helps others for no pay

   (a) a telemarketer   (b) a volunteer

5. goods and services we give to people in need

   (a) donations and contributions   (b) flyers and letters

F. Write a response. Use your own words.

"Telemarketers keep calling me during dinner. I need advice." _____

_____

G. Composition. On a separate sheet of paper, write about the picture on page 12. Say as much as you can.

> **Now I can**
> ❑ agree to contribute to a good cause.
> ❑ decline a telemarketer's sales solicitation.
> ❑ understand the spirit of volunteerism.
> ❑ avoid telemarketing fraud.

The community

Preview

Warm up. Look at this section of a lease. What is a lease for? Have you ever signed a lease?

PESTS. Lessee is responsible for maintaining the premises free of pests and shall pay for any desired pest control services.

UTILITIES. Lessee shall pay all utilities, except when noted, upon the subject premises for the entire term of this Lease agreement. Lessee shall cause all utilities to be transferred to his/her name at the beginning of the Lease period. If Lessee shall fail to do so or should Lessee fail to pay any utility, Lessee shall be liable for any and all said charges and in addition shall also be liable to Lessor for a fee in the amount of $25 for each month or part thereof that this occurs as reimbursement for Lessor's time and expense incurred.

Unit 2 objectives

- Describe a housing emergency.
- Ask for housing repairs.
- Know what to look for in a potential rental.
- Understand tenant rights.
- Understand the Fair Housing Act.
- Act on housing discrimination.

Practical conversations

Model 1   Ask for an emergency repair.

A. Listen and read.

A: I've got an emergency in my apartment.
B: What's the problem?
A: There's no heat.
B: I can look at that tomorrow.
A: I'm sorry. But this is urgent.
B: OK. I'll see what I can do.

B. Pronunciation and intonation practice.

Vocabulary

Household emergencies

A pipe burst.

The lock is broken.

The window is broken.

There's no heat.

There's no hot water.

There's no air conditioning.

C. Pair work. Ask for an emergency repair.

A: I've got an emergency in my apartment.
B: What's the problem?
A: _____.
B: I can look at that _____.
A: I'm sorry. But this is urgent.
B: _____.

A. Listen and read.

A: Hi, Peter. How's it going?

B: Not great. Our cable's out. Is yours out too?

A: I hope not. I'll check and let you know.

B: Thanks.

B. Pronunciation and intonation practice.

Vocabulary

Utilities

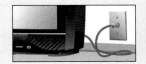         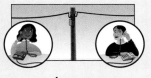

cable   power   gas   phones

C. Pair work. Tell another tenant in your building about an outage.

A: Hi, _____. _____?

B: _____. _____ out. _____ yours out too?

A: I hope not. I'll check and let you know.

B: _____.

➤ Do it yourself!

A. Pair work. **Create a conversation for the tenant and the building manager.**

B. Discussion. **Have you ever had an emergency in your own house or apartment? What did you do about it?**

I called the building manager.

I called a plumber.

I called an electrician.

I fixed it myself.

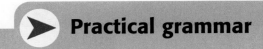

Practical grammar

The present perfect

Form the present perfect with *have* or *has* and a past participle.

> She **hasn't paid** the rent yet.

Use the present perfect with *ever, never, already, still,* and *yet* for actions that have happened before now—if the exact time is not stated or not important, as in these examples.

> **Have** you *ever* **signed** a lease?
> She's *never* **had** an emergency in her house.
> I've *already* **seen** that apartment.
> We **haven't signed** the lease *yet*. They **haven't** either.

Do not use the present perfect when a time is stated. Use the simple past tense for actions that happened at a stated time in the past.

> I **signed** it yesterday. (before now—exact time is stated) NOT: ~~I have signed it yesterday.~~

A. Complete the paragraph with the present perfect.

I _____ thirty apartments in this city! I _____
       1. see   **2.** look at

every school and I _____ the shops and services in every neighborhood
                             3. check

where I _____ renting an apartment. But I still _____
           4. think about   **5.** not find

the right one! I _____ a neighborhood that has a good elementary
                     6. not be in

school that my children can walk to, a good selection of inexpensive restaurants, and

stores that stay open late. I _____ in many cities, but now I have
                                 7. live

to live here, and I _____ any luck yet.
                     8. not have

B. Complete each sentence with the present perfect or the simple past tense.

1. I _____ that apartment on Monday.
      have seen / saw

2. My husband _____ the manager about the hot water.
      already notified / has already notified

3. He _____ me back yet.
      didn't call / hasn't called

4. The maintenance staff _____ this morning.
      came / has come

5. Our cable _____ out. _____ yours?
      was never / has never been   Was / Has

For and *since*

Use the present perfect with *for* or *since* for actions that started in the past and continue in the present.
> I've **lived** here *since 2002*. (I still live here.)
> Ms. Drake **has been** our landlord *for ten years*. (She's still our landlord.)
With *for* or *since*, the present perfect continuous has the same meaning as the present perfect.
> I've **been living** here *since 2002* = I've **lived** here *since 2002*.

C. **Complete the paragraph about actions that started in the past with *for* or *since*.**

Mr. Clark has been a tenant at 33 Riverside Drive _____ April.
1.

But he has lived in New York _____ over ten years. Mr. Clark has
2.

worked at the Starburst Room of the Claremont Hotel _____ 1998.
3.

He has been an executive chef _____ only the last year.
4.

➤ Do it yourself!

A. **Complete the housing history form about yourself.**

Green Tree Properties _____ Application and Housing History

Your name _____

What is your current address? _____

How long have you lived at that address? _____

Where did you live before that? _____

B. **Role play. Role-play a conversation between a rental agent and a tenant applying for an apartment. Use the information in your housing history.**

How long have you lived there?

I've lived on 11th Street since 1999.

Unit 2   **19**

Authentic practice

Renting a house or apartment

A. Read the picture story again. Then check *True* or *False* for each statement.

	True	False
1. Landlords are always responsible for repairs.	❏	❏
2. If the tenant breaks a window, the tenant has to pay for the repair.	❏	❏
3. Tenants are always permitted to sublet their apartments.	❏	❏
4. Tenants can sublet for two years.	❏	❏
5. The man asks for more time.	❏	❏

B. Listen. Read each response out loud from the text.

C. Vocabulary. Choose one of the words or phrases to complete each sentence.

1. _____ is letting another person live in your apartment and pay
   <u>Subletting / Leasing</u>

   the rent when you are not there.

2. A _____ is a legal contract between a tenant and a landlord.
   <u>utility / lease</u>

3. "You are _____ for payment" means you have to pay.
   <u>responsible / included</u>

4. _____ are basic services that tenants need.
   <u>Sublets / Utilities</u>

5. A flood or a fire can cause _____.
   <u>damage / approval</u>

6. When you cause a problem, you are _____.
   <u>at fault / fair</u>

7. Tenants have to get their landlord's _____ before subletting.
   <u>lease / approval</u>

D. Read each question. Underline your response.

1. "What's the policy on repairs?"

   YOU If you break it, you fix it.   **YOU** Fair enough.

2. "Do you know the terms on sublets?"

   YOU Only if you're at fault.   **YOU** Not off the top of my head. I'll check.

3. "Do you mind if I ask you a few more questions?"

   YOU Absolutely not.   **YOU** Is that a problem?

E. Pair work. Take turns reading the items and responses in Exercise D.

➤ Do it yourself!

Write your own response. Then read the conversation out loud with a partner.

If you are at fault for any damage, you'll be responsible for the repair.   **YOU** _____

I don't know the answer off the top of my head. Can I get back to you on that?   **YOU** _____

Any other questions about the lease?   **YOU** _____

Tips for apartment hunters

a dead-bolt lock   a circuit breaker   a switch   a mouse trap

a bait trap   roaches

🎧 **A. Listening comprehension. Listen to the radio call-in show about renting an apartment or a house. Take notes on a separate sheet of paper as you listen.**

B. Answer the questions in your own words.

1. Who are Jack Mee and Irene from Moline? _____

2. What does Irene want to know about? _____

3. Jack Mee offers a lot of advice. In your opinion, which piece of advice is most important? _____

C. Pair work. Compare answers with a partner.

🎧 **D. Which subjects does Jack Mee give tips about? Listen again and then check the boxes.**

1. ☐ street lighting
2. ☐ plumbing
3. ☐ appliances
4. ☐ noise

5. ☐ electrical wiring
6. ☐ pest infestation
7. ☐ maintenance
8. ☐ laundry facilities

E. Vocabulary. Match each term in column A with a related term in column B.

A	B
_f_ 1. security	a. smoke detectors
____ 2. fire code	b. trash
____ 3. electrical wiring	c. bait traps
____ 4. pest infestation	d. fuses and circuit breakers
____ 5. common area neglect	e. burners
____ 6. appliances	f. dead-bolt locks

F. Complete the self-test about your house or apartment.

	yes	no
1 Do you feel safe in the neighborhood?	○	○
2 Do you feel safe in your apartment?	○	○
3 Does your door have dead-bolt locks?	○	○
4 Do your appliances work?	○	○
5 Do you have laundry facilities in the building?	○	○

G. True story. Tell your partner about your neighborhood and your apartment or house. Use your self-test for ideas.

FYI. A good place to look for apartments is this helpful Web site:

http://www.apartments.about.com/library/tools/bl_huntingchecklist.htm

Other places to look for an apartment:
- Ads posted on supermarket bulletin boards
- Real estate agencies
- Classified ads in the local newspaper
- Word of mouth

➤ Do it yourself!

A. Write a list of questions to ask a rental agent or building superintendent about an apartment or a house you are interested in.

Questions
1. *Is there a laundry room?*
2.
3.
4.

B. Pair work. Use the questions to create a role play between a tenant and a rental agent or building superintendent.

Fair housing and equal opportunity

A. Read about the Fair Housing Act.

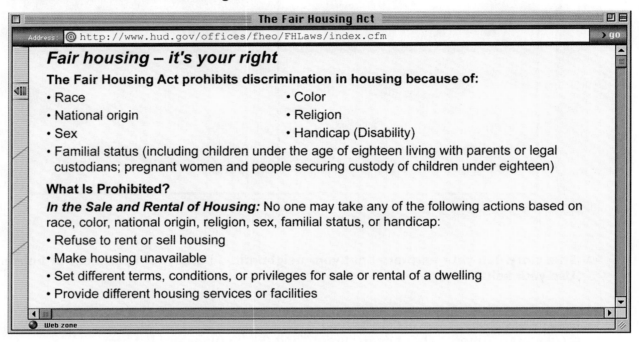

The Fair Housing Act

Address: @ http://www.hud.gov/offices/fheo/FHLaws/index.cfm ⟩ go

Fair housing – it's your right
The Fair Housing Act prohibits discrimination in housing because of:
- Race
- Color
- National origin
- Religion
- Sex
- Handicap (Disability)
- Familial status (including children under the age of eighteen living with parents or legal custodians; pregnant women and people securing custody of children under eighteen)

What Is Prohibited?
In the Sale and Rental of Housing: No one may take any of the following actions based on race, color, national origin, religion, sex, familial status, or handicap:
- Refuse to rent or sell housing
- Make housing unavailable
- Set different terms, conditions, or privileges for sale or rental of a dwelling
- Provide different housing services or facilities

Web zone

B. Vocabulary. Read the definitions. Then complete each sentence with one of the words.

a. **an act:** a law
b. **a right:** a legal permission
c. **prohibit:** not permit, prevent
d. **refuse:** not give permission
e. **disability:** a physical or mental condition that makes everyday actions difficult; for example, being hearing impaired

f. **discrimination:** illegally refusing to treat certain people equal to others because of a difference or disability
g. **a complaint:** a legal document that says a person has been unlawfully discriminated against
h. **a dwelling:** a place to live—a house or an apartment

1. We filed a _____ when the landlord said we couldn't have the
   complaint / discrimination

   apartment because we have two young children.

2. It's my _____ to rent an apartment, no matter what my religion is.
   act / right

3. Although I have a _____, the landlord can't refuse to rent me
   dwelling / disability

   an apartment.

4. This apartment lease _____ pets. It has a no-pet policy.
   prohibits / permits

C. Critical thinking. Read the case studies. Did the landlord commit a violation?

Chen

1. Warren Chen is blind. He has a specially trained dog that helps him in his daily activities outside of his home. He has an appointment to talk about renting an apartment. When he arrives for the appointment, the landlord says she's sorry, but the apartment has a no-pet policy.

Martin

2. Jolie Martin makes an appointment to see an apartment. When the rental agent learns that she is Haitian, he tells her that the unit is unavailable and that the building is full.

Hasan

3. Mohammad Hasan calls and leaves a message that he would like to see a house that is advertised in the local paper. The office doesn't call him back to make an appointment. Mr. Hasan suspects that the landlord doesn't want to rent to Muslims, so he calls again about the same apartment but leaves another name. The landlord calls back immediately and makes an appointment.

Johnson

4. Marjorie Johnson wants to rent an apartment. When she arrives to see it, the landlord tells her that the apartment is no longer available.

Schwartz

5. Milton Schwartz is a single father with six children. He wants an apartment with three bedrooms. The landlord says he doesn't have an apartment that big.

D. Discussion. Explain your answers in Exercise C to your group or partner. Use the Fair Housing Act on page 24 for support. (To download an official complaint form from the U.S. Department of Housing and Urban Development (HUD), click on www.hud.gov.)

➤ Do it yourself!

A. Discussion. Discuss the questions about housing rights in your home country.

1. Do landlords sometimes discriminate against tenants who want to rent?

2. Are tenants protected by the law?

3. What are some of the ways in which landlords discriminate? For instance, do they discriminate on the basis of language, religion, disability, or other?

B. Culture talk. Compare and contrast information about housing rights in your home country and your classmates' countries.

⌒ B. Listening comprehension. Listen to the conversations. Then decide what the problems are. Fill in the ovals.

1. ⓐ an electrical problem   ⓑ a flood
2. ⓐ a security problem   ⓑ a plumbing problem
3. ⓐ a cable outage   ⓑ a gas outage
4. ⓐ a safety problem   ⓑ pest infestation
5. ⓐ housing discrimination   ⓑ a lease problem

C. Read each sentence or question. Underline your response.

1. "The cable's out."

   YOU But my favorite show is on tonight!   **YOU** That's a violation of the Fair Housing Act!

2. "Have you checked all the burners?"

   YOU Yes, and there's a pest problem.   **YOU** Yes, the stove is fine.

3. "What are the terms of the lease?"

   YOU It's for two years, and it permits sublets.   **YOU** It's out again.

4. "But how secure is the apartment?"

   YOU Well, there's a dead-bolt lock on both doors.   **YOU** Well, I didn't see any traps or sprays.

5. "Do you think you were discriminated against?"

   YOU I'm not sure. I'll call the manager.   **YOU** I'm not sure. I need to check the Fair Housing Act.

6. "Do you know which utilities are included?"

   YOU Not off the top of my head.   **YOU** Plumbing and electrical problems, I think.

7. "Who's at fault for this water damage?"

   YOU It has a no-pet policy.   **YOU** The tenant.

D. Complete each sentence with the present perfect or the simple present tense.

1. Last year I _____ to rent an apartment in this building.
   tried / have tried

2. This morning, the landlord _____ me that I need a new lease.
   told / has told

3. I _____ in such a terrible apartment.
   never lived / have never lived

4. The locks are broken. I called the manager, but he _____ yet.
   didn't call me back / hasn't called me back

5. I _____ for another apartment.
   already looked / have already looked

6. It's hard to move. I _____ here for a long time.
   lived / have lived

E. Choose one or more of the questions. Find the information in the unit and write the answer in your own words.

1. What is an outage? _____

   _____

2. What is a lease? _____

   _____

3. What is a disability? _____

   _____

4. What is illegal discrimination?

   _____

F. Composition. On a separate sheet of paper, write about the picture on page 26. Say as much as you can.

> **Now I can**
> ❏ describe a housing emergency.
> ❏ ask for housing repairs.
> ❏ know what to look for in a potential rental.
> ❏ understand tenant rights.
> ❏ understand the Fair Housing Act.
> ❏ act on housing discrimination.

Technology

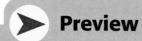

Preview

Warm up. Do you have all the "should haves" in your car? Have you ever needed to use this equipment?

Road Talk Magazine/July 2004   67

THE RESPONSIBLE DRIVER

Emergencies can happen at a moment's notice and can turn deadly in an instant. We can't plan for emergencies, but we can be equipped to handle them. This month, the Responsible Driver examines what you should have in your car at all times. Better safe than sorry!

"Should haves" self-check

Check the items you have in your car right now. Then get the ones you don't have ASAP! Common sense requires that you have these items in your car in case of a breakdown or in case you have to assist another driver in need.

- ❑ a flashlight with working batteries—keep some spares!
- ❑ a spare tire—to replace a flat tire
- ❑ a jack—to change the tire
- ❑ flares—to warn oncoming traffic that you are stopped
- ❑ jumper cables—to start a car with a dead battery

Unit 3 objectives

- Respond appropriately to a police officer in a traffic stop.
- Describe an accident.
- Understand traffic violations.
- Avoid aggressive driving and road rage.
- Drive by the Golden Rule.
- Understand what equipment is needed in a car.

Practical conversations

Model 1 Respond appropriately in a traffic stop.

A. Listen and read.

A: I'm going to have to give you a ticket for speeding.

B: You're right. I'm sorry, officer.

A: License and registration, please.

B: Here you go.

A: I'll be back in a few minutes. Please turn off your engine.

B: OK.

B. Pronunciation and intonation practice.

Vocabulary

Traffic violations

speeding

not stopping at a stop sign

not yielding at a yield sign

tailgating

not signaling

talking on a hand-held cell phone

C. Pair work. Get a ticket for a traffic violation.

A: I'm going to have to give you a ticket for _____.

B: You're right. I'm sorry, officer.

A: License and registration, please.

B: _____.

A: I'll be back in a few minutes. Please turn off your engine.

B: _____.

🎧**A.** **Listen and read.**

> **A:** I had an accident. I sideswiped another car.
> **B:** Oh, no. Was anyone hurt?
> **A:** No, thank goodness. It was just a fender bender, but I'm really upset.
> **B:** Well, take it easy. The insurance will cover it.

🎧**B.** **Pronunciation and intonation practice.**

🎧 **Reactions to accidents**

It was just a fender bender, but I'm really upset.
But there was a lot of damage, and I'm really upset.

🎧 **Vocabulary**

Car accidents

I **sideswiped** a parked car.

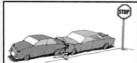

I was following too closely, and I **rear-ended** another car.

I **totaled** the car.

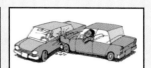

I wasn't paying attention, and I **hit** another car.

C. **Pair work.** **Discuss an accident.**

> **A:** I had an accident. I _____.
> **B:** Oh, no. Was anyone hurt?
> **A:** No, thank goodness. _____.
> **B:** _____. The insurance will cover it.

➤ Do it yourself!

A. **True story.** **Describe an accident you had or an accident you know about. What was the cause?**

Accident	What was the cause?
a fender bender	The driver was talking on a cell phone.

B. **Pair work.** **Compare information with your partner.**

C. **Discussion.** **Bring in an article describing an accident from a newspaper. Discuss the accident with your classmates. What happened? What was the cause?**

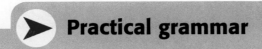

Practical grammar

Using gerunds

> A gerund is the *-ing* form of the verb, used as a noun. Gerunds can be used in a variety of ways.
>
> as a subject of a sentence:
>> **Passing** on the right is dangerous.
>
> as an object of a verb:
>> I don't like **honking** at another driver.
>
> as an object of a preposition:
>> Even if you're in a hurry, that's no excuse for **speeding**.
>
> as a complement:
>> My favorite way to get places is **driving**.

See page 146 for a list of verbs followed by gerunds. See page 147 for how to spell the gerund and the present participle.

A. Complete the sentences with gerunds.

1. We got a ticket for not _____ at the stop sign.

stop

2. _____ the scene of an accident is a serious crime.

Leave

3. The officer stopped us for not _____ to the car in the rotary.

yield

4. _____ is not permitted in a bus stop.

Park

5. I get angry at drivers for _____.

tailgate

6. I'm not used to _____ at night.

drive

7. The worst traffic offense is _____.

speed

8. _____ on a hand-held cell phone while driving is very distracting

Talk
   to a driver.

9. I'm tired of _____ tickets. I'd better stop _____ so

get   *drive*
   fast!

10. Instead of _____ the speed limit, he just kept _____

observe   *look*
    for radar traps.

Infinitives of purpose

An infinitive is *to* and the simple form of the verb. Infinitives are used after certain verbs: *decide, forget, need, plan, remember, want.*

   Remember **to pass** on the left, not on the right.

You can use an infinitive to explain the purpose of an action. Statements using an infinitive of purpose often answer questions with *why*.

   A: And why did the officer stop you?
   B: **To give** me a ticket.

See page 146 for a list of verbs followed by infinitives.

B. **Read Dr. Jamie Greene's "to-do" list for tomorrow. Then answer the questions with an infinitive of purpose.**

> renew my driver's license
>
> make an appointment with the guidance counselor about college visits for Sam
>
> buy new tires
>
> pay my parking ticket
>
> pick up cookies for the office party

1. Why did she drive to the Department of Motor Vehicles? *to renew her driver's license*

2. Why did she call the guidance counselor?

   _____

3. Why did she drive to Discount Tire World?

   _____

4. Why did she go to the municipal courthouse? _____

5. Why did she drive to the bakery? _____

C. **Complete each answer. Use an infinitive of purpose.**

1. Why do police officers stop speeders? They stop speeders *to give them tickets.*

2. Why do people speed? They speed _____

   _____.

3. Why did you get a driver's license? I got a driver's license _____

   _____.

➤ Do it yourself!

A. **Make a list of where you went yesterday and why. Use infinitives of purpose.**

Activity	Purpose
I went to the ATM	to get money for groceries

B. **Pair work. Ask your partner what he or she did yesterday. Ask why.**

Authentic practice

Appropriate behavior with a police officer

A. **Read the picture story again. Answer the questions.**

1. Why did the officer pull the driver over? _____

2. What did the officer ask for? _____

3. How fast was the driver driving? _____

B. **Vocabulary. Choose one of the words or phrases to complete each sentence.**

1. Uh-oh! There's a cop behind us with her lights flashing. I think she's going to
   _____!
   <u>let us off / pull us over</u>

2. I'm sorry, _____. I didn't realize how fast I was going.
   <u>cop / officer</u>

3. Are you aware that I _____ you going over 80?
   <u>warned / clocked</u>

4. Be sure to look both ways before you _____. There's a lot of traffic.
   <u>are wise / pull out</u>

5. This time I'm going to _____. Next time it'll be more serious.
   <u>pull you over / let you off</u>

34   Unit 3

⌢ **C.** **Listen. Read each response out loud from the text on page 34.**

D. **Read each sentence or question. Underline your response.**

1. "Do you know why I pulled you over?"

   (**YOU**) Yes, officer. I was speeding.   (**YOU**) Yes, officer. To clock me.

2. "Are you aware how fast you were going?"

   (**YOU**) To get to the bank.   (**YOU**) Actually, no. I'm sorry.

3. "Being in a hurry is no excuse."

   (**YOU**) I know. You're right.   (**YOU**) As a matter of fact.

4. "I'm going to let you off easy this time."

   (**YOU**) I really appreciate it, officer.   (**YOU**) It was just a fender bender.

5. "Be careful when you pull out. "

   (**YOU**) I sideswiped the car.   (**YOU**) I will. Thanks for the warning.

E. **Pair work. Take turns reading the items and responses in Exercise D.**

> ## ➤ Do it yourself!

A. **Write your own response. Then read the conversation out loud with a partner.**

 I'm going to have to see your license and registration.   (**YOU**) _____

 You were tailgating, and then you didn't signal your right turn.   (**YOU**) _____

 You got off easy this time. Next time you might not be so lucky.   (**YOU**) _____

B. **Culture talk. In the country you come from, what are some traffic violations? What are the penalties for committing them? What do you say to a police officer who stops you? Compare cultures with your classmates.**

Authentic practice

Aggressive driving and road rage

🎧 **A.** Listening comprehension. Listen to the panel discussion.

B. Discussion. Answer the question. Then discuss with the class.

What's the difference between aggressive driving and road rage? _____

_____

🎧 **C.** Listen to the panel discussion again. Check the advice given to help people avoid the consequences of road rage.

1. ☐ Get angry.
2. ☐ Step back from your anger.
3. ☐ Go to the Behavior Management Institute.

4. ☐ Control others.
5. ☐ Recognize you can't control others.
6. ☐ Don't take things personally.

D. Look at the examples of aggressive driving.

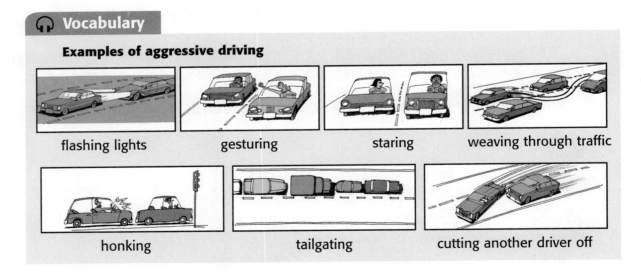

🎧 **Vocabulary**

Examples of aggressive driving

flashing lights   gesturing   staring   weaving through traffic

honking   tailgating   cutting another driver off

E. Discussion. What's your reaction to aggressive driving?

I honk back!

I don't do anything. It's not worth looking for trouble.

I don't take it personally.

36   Unit 3

➤ Do it yourself!

A. Complete the magazine survey about driver attitudes.

What's your driving anger quotient?

The National Highway Transportation Safety Administration estimates that aggressive driving has caused **2.28 million accidents** and **27,935 deaths** in the past five years. Aggressive driving is often a response to feeling stress and getting angry at the driving of others.

How do these behaviors affect you?
Rate each behavior on a scale of 1 to 3.

| 1 = not bothered | 2 = annoyed | 3 = very angry |

Circle the number after each behavior.

HOT-BUTTON BEHAVIORS

1.	Tailgating to make others go faster or get out of the way	1	2	3
2.	Flashing lights to signal others to move to another lane	1	2	3
3.	Making hand gestures at others	1	2	3
4.	Weaving in and out of traffic	1	2	3
5.	Honking excessively	1	2	3
6.	Driving too slowly in the passing lane so no one can pass	1	2	3
7.	Staring angrily at another driver	1	2	3
8.	Cutting people off	1	2	3
9.	Slowing down after passing someone	1	2	3
10.	Trying to beat a yellow light that's about to turn red	1	2	3
11.	Not making a right turn in the right-hand turn lane	1	2	3
12.	Not reacting quickly after the red light turns green	1	2	3

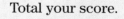

Total your score.

What your score means

30-36: Calm down. Life is shorter than you think.

24-29: Don't let the behavior of others have power over you.

12-23: You're cool as a cucumber.

B. Collaborative activity. Compile the scores of all the students in the class.

C. Culture talk. How do people feel about these behaviors in the country you come from? Does driving behavior differ from country to country? Compare cultures.

Driving by the Golden Rule

A. Read and listen to the letters.

Ask Joan

Culture tips for newcomers

Dear Joan:
The other day I was driving out of a parking lot and my baby was in the back seat. She threw down her bottle, and for a second I was distracted. I reached back to get her bottle and I bumped a little into another car. It was just a soft bump, but I was afraid to stop to look, Joan, so I drove away. I don't have a lot of money and every little scratch and dent costs so much to fix. My wife said I did the wrong thing. She told me to think how angry I would be if someone hit my car and caused damage and didn't leave a name and phone number for me to call. What do you think?

Clarence in Claremont

Dear Clarence:
I'm with your wife on this one. And

so is the law. It's against the law to leave the scene of an accident, even a small one, if there is any property damage. But over and above the law, put yourself in the shoes of the owner of the car and you will understand why leaving was wrong. There's nothing you can do now, but let this be a lesson to you and to all my readers.

Joan

Dear Joan:
Last week I saw a car parked on the shoulder of the road and it looked like the driver might be sick. I wanted to stop to help him, but a passenger in my car said I would just be looking for trouble. He told me that if I stopped to help and the man died or something else bad happened, that his family could go to court to sue me. Joan, it seems like everybody in this country wants to go to court to sue someone! I didn't stop, but I still feel bad about it.

Lucille from Louisiana

Dear Lucille:
If you see a person in imminent danger of dying, and your actions could save that person's life, you should not be afraid to stop and help.

The laws everywhere protect "Good Samaritans" from being sued under such circumstances. Under more normal circumstances, however, where there is no immediate danger of death, the best advice is to call 911 from a car phone or from the most convenient public or emergency phone. In that way, trained medical personnel will arrive quickly.

Remember, though, the courts expect people to behave with common sense. No one expects you to be a doctor or to have medical training. It's always best to drive (and live!) by the Golden Rule: Treat others as you wish others to treat you.

Joan

B. Read the letters again. Then answer the questions.

1. Why didn't Clarence stop? _____

2. What did Lucille see? _____

3. Why didn't she stop? _____

4. What is the Golden Rule? _____

C. Pair work. What advice would you give to each driver? Compare advice with a partner.

Uh-oh. I might have sideswiped that parked car. I don't think anything happened, though. And anyway, the owner isn't there.

Look at the woman in that parked car over there. Do you think there's something wrong? She's got her head down on the wheel.

YOU _____

YOU _____

D. Read the car equipment safety checklist from *Road Talk Magazine.*

Road Talk Magazine / July 2004

THE RESPONSIBLE DRIVER

Emergencies can happen at a moment's notice and can turn deadly in an instant. We can't plan for emergencies, but we can be equipped to handle them. This month, the Responsible Driver examines what you should have in your car at all times. Better safe than sorry!

"Should haves" self-check
Check the items you have in your car right now. Then get the ones you don't have ASAP! Common sense requires that you have these items in your car in case of a breakdown or in case you have to assist another driver in need.

- ❑ a flashlight with working batteries—keep some spares!
- ❑ a spare tire—to replace a flat tire
- ❑ a jack—to change the tire
- ❑ flares—to warn oncoming traffic that you are stopped
- ❑ jumper cables—to start a car with a dead battery

"Must haves"
And don't forget these! The law requires that you have these items in your car in case of an accident or a police stop.

- ❑ car registration—to establish the name of the owner of the car and the state the car is registered in
- ❑ insurance card—to provide to any driver whose car you might have damaged, to show who to contact about the damages
- ❑ your valid driver's license—of course!

E. Critical thinking. **Look in the trunk of each car. What should the driver get?**

Get today: _____   Get today: _____

➤ Do it yourself!

A. True story. **Tell a true car story to your partner or your group. Choose one of these topics:**

- an accident
- a ticket
- an experience with an aggressive driver or road rage
- a problem with a car
- car equipment

B. Discussion. **What was the problem? What happened? What was the solution?**

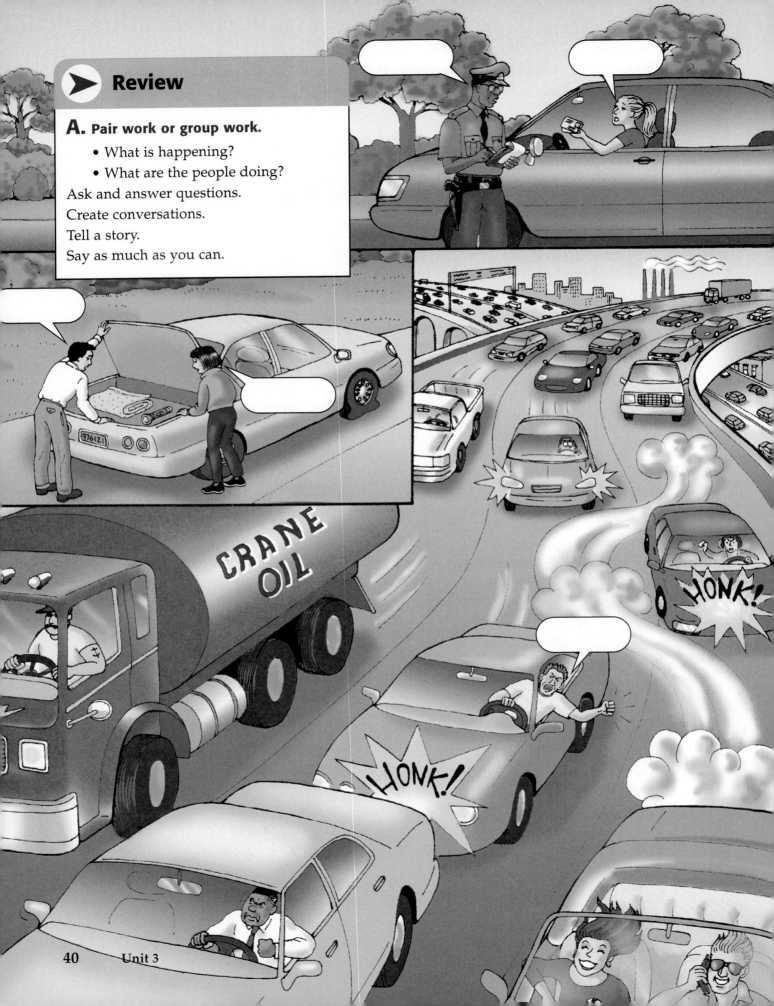

Review

A. Pair work or group work.

- What is happening?
- What are the people doing?

Ask and answer questions.

Create conversations.

Tell a story.

Say as much as you can.

B. Listening comprehension. Listen to the conversation between a father and his teenage daughter. Check the equipment they have and the equipment they need.

	They have	They need
1. License	❑	❑
2. Registration	❑	❑
3. Insurance card	❑	❑
4. Spare tire	❑	❑
5. Jack	❑	❑
6. Flashlight	❑	❑
7. Flares	❑	❑
8. Jumper cables	❑	❑

C. Read each sentence or question. Underline your response.

1. "Do you know why I pulled you over?"

   YOU No, thank goodness.   **YOU** I think I was tailgating.

2. "You were speeding. I clocked you at 84."

   YOU You're right. I was going a little fast.   **YOU** Take it easy.

3. "You're getting off easy this time. Next time it's a ticket and points."

   YOU That's no excuse.   **YOU** I appreciate it, officer.

4. "Leave yourself a little extra time so you won't have to speed."

   YOU That's a good idea.   **YOU** Be careful when you pull out.

D. Complete each sentence with the name of the equipment.

jumper cables	spare	jack	registration	flare

1. You need a _____ to change a flat tire.

2. If you have a flat tire, you need to replace it with a _____.

3. When you have an accident and are stopped on the side of the road, protect yourself from other motorists by lighting a _____.

4. Be sure to carry _____ to help start a car that has a dead battery.

5. Two important documents that you should always have with you when you drive are an insurance card and the car's _____.

E. Read about the equipment. Then complete each sentence with a phrase using an infinitive of purpose.

🎧 **Vocabulary**

Emergency use of equipment

a flashlight—**helps you look under the hood in the dark**

a blanket—**keeps you warm if you break down on a cold night**

a cell phone—**enables you to call for service in an emergency**

a map—**helps you find places when you don't have directions**

an auto club membership—**provides free or inexpensive emergency road service**

1. I have a flashlight *to help me look under the hood in the dark* .

2. I have a blanket _____ .

3. I have a cell phone _____ .

4. I have maps _____ .

5. I belong to an auto club _____ .

F. Complete the sentences with gerunds.

1. I got a ticket for not _____ at the light.
                              stop

2. I can't stand aggressive _____ .
                              drive

3. The subject of the magazine article is _____ road rage.
                                             avoid

4. _____ others' behavior is impossible.
   Control

G. Composition. On a separate sheet of paper, write about the picture on page 40.

Now I can
❑ respond appropriately to a police officer in a traffic stop.
❑ describe an accident.
❑ understand traffic violations.
❑ avoid aggressive driving and road rage.
❑ drive by the Golden Rule.
❑ understand what equipment is needed in a car.

The consumer world

> **Preview**

Warm up. Do you believe this offer is true? Explain your answer.

You have been specially selected!

U.S. POSTAGE

H METER 1234567

Hello... you have been specially selected to receive our SPECTACULAR LUXURY DREAM VACATION offer!

Unit 4 objectives

- Request service and respond to requests for service.
- Make and respond to complaints about bad service.
- Make and guarantee hotel reservations.
- Check in at a hotel.
- Evaluate offers for vacation packages.
- Protect yourself against travel fraud.

Practical conversations

🎧 **A.** **Listen and read.**

A: Front desk. May I help you?

B: Hello. This is Mr. Hasan in Room 403. Would it be possible to get an ironing board?

A: Absolutely, Mr. Hasan. Right away. Is there anything else?

B: Actually, I could use some extra towels too.

A: Sure, no problem.

🎧 **B.** **Pronunciation and intonation practice.**

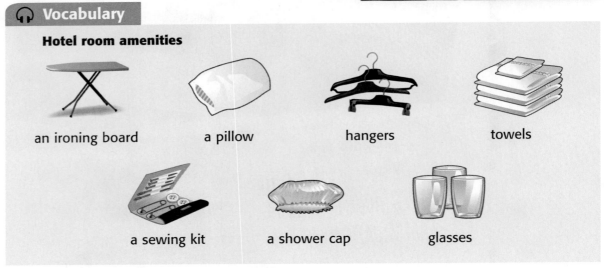

🎧 **Vocabulary**

Hotel room amenities

an ironing board   a pillow   hangers   towels

a sewing kit   a shower cap   glasses

C. Pair work. **Ask the front desk to send you something you need. Use the items in the vocabulary and in the box, or other items you would like.**

| shampoo | conditioner | a sewing kit | washcloths |
| soap | lotion | a shower cap | glasses |

A: Front desk. _____?

B: Hello. This is _____ in Room _____. Would it be possible to get _____?

A: Absolutely, _____. Right away. Is there anything else?

B: Actually, I could use _____ too.

A: _____.

44   Unit 4

A. Listen and read.

A: I have a complaint. I ordered breakfast from room service, and it never came.

B: I'm so sorry. Is there some way we can make that up to you?

A: Well, just make sure it's not on my bill.

B: Of course. And please accept my apology.

B. Pronunciation and intonation practice.

Vocabulary

Hotel services

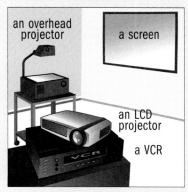

an overhead projector

a screen

an LCD projector

a VCR

audiovisual equipment

photocopies

a meal

a newspaper

beverages

C. Pair work. Complain about service. Use the hotel departments in the box.

room service	the business center	the catering department
the front desk	the gift shop	the housekeeping department

A: I have a complaint. I ordered _____ and _____.

B: I'm so sorry. Is there some way we can make that up to you?

A: _____.

B: _____. And please accept my apology.

➤ Do it yourself!

A. What's important to you in a hotel or motel? Rate the following items from 1 (least important) to 5 (most important).

- price _____
- location _____
- service _____
- amenities _____

I like a hotel near the center of the city because I don't want to spend a lot on taxis.

B. Discussion. Explain your opinions to your partner or your group.

Practical grammar

Use *some* and *any* to describe an indefinite amount or number (exact amount or number not known).

Use *some* in affirmative statements.

They brought us **some** extra soap.

Now we have **some**.

Use *any* in negative statements.

We don't want **any** lotion, and we don't need **any** towels.

They don't have **any**. (*Any* could refer to the lotion or the towels.)

Use *some* or *any* in questions.

Do you need **some** extra cups or shampoo?

Do you need **any** extra cups or shampoo?

A. Rewrite the affirmative sentences in the negative.

1. There is some ice in the bucket.

   There isn't any ice in the bucket.

2. There are some towels in the housekeeper's closet.

   _____

3. We have some extra shampoo for you.

   _____

4. The women need some skirt hangers.

   _____

5. She left some luggage at the bell desk.

   _____

6. There's some problem with the phones in their suite.

   _____

7. He has some laundry to pick up.

   _____

8. I need some help with the audiovisual equipment.

   _____

9. Please send some butter up with my breakfast.

   _____

B. Complete each statement with *some* or *any*.

1. I don't want _____ more coffee, thank you.

2. There isn't _____ soap in the bathroom.

3. They asked for _____ assistance with their luggage.

4. The business center is making _____ copies of this flyer.

5. You didn't order _____ dessert?

6. It's a shame that there isn't _____ cable service in the room.

7. I don't see _____ request for breakfast for Room 203.

8. There are _____ phone messages for you on the desk.

C. Write *yes–no* questions with *some* or *any*.

1. there is / cold food on the menu / ?

   _____

2. there are / newspapers in the gift shop / ?

   _____

3. you / need / extra towels / ?

   _____

4. they / want / milk with their coffee / ?

   _____

5. Ms. Banks / need / help with her luggage / ?

   _____

6. the housekeeping department / have / more hangers / ?

   _____

➤ Do it yourself!

Pair work. Look at the picture of the kitchen for one minute. Then close the book and ask questions about the things in the room. Use *Is there*, *Are there*, and *some* and *any* in your questions. Answer from memory.

Is there any fruit?

Authentic practice

The hotel check-in

A. Read the picture story again. Then check *True* or *False* for each statement.

	True	False
1. Ms. Thompson is checking out of the hotel.	☐	☐
2. Ms. Thompson is paying her hotel bill.	☐	☐
3. Ms. Thompson asked for a key to the mini-bar.	☐	☐
4. Ms. Thompson has luggage.	☐	☐

B. Check the information the clerk requests.

1. ☐ length of stay
2. ☐ check-out date
3. ☐ check-in time
4. ☐ need for bellman assistance

C. Listen. Read each response out loud from the text.

D. **Vocabulary. Choose one of the words or phrases to complete each sentence.**

1. Would it be possible to make _____ for a non-smoking double
   facing the ocean?
   <u>a reservation / an imprint</u>

2. That room won't be _____. I requested a non-smoking room.
   <u>satisfactory / available</u>

3. I have a lot of _____. I'm going to need some help.
   <u>luggage / bellmen</u>

4. I'm traveling with my daughter, so I need a _____.
   <u>single / double</u>

E. **Find and write the four questions the clerk asked when Ms. Thompson checked in.**

_____

_____

_____

F. **Role play. Role-play a conversation between a traveler checking in and a front desk hotel clerk. Use the questions you wrote in Exercise E and your own questions.**

G. **Reread the picture story on page 48. Write what you know about Ms. Thompson.**

She's married. _____

_____

➤ Do it yourself!

A. **Read the hotel guests' statements. Write your own responses. Then read each conversation out loud with a partner.**

I have a lot of audiovisual equipment to carry.

YOU _____

I wanted a double room, but the key you gave me is for a single.

YOU _____

The key to the mini-bar doesn't work.

YOU _____

B. **Discussion. What other problems can the front desk help travelers with?**

Authentic practice

A. Listening comprehension. Listen to the telephone conversation.

B. Discussion. Answer the questions. Then compare your answers.

1. Who made the phone call and why? _____

2. Why does the man give his credit card number to the woman? _____

_____

C. Look at the hotel reservations form on the computer screen. Then listen to the conversation again. Fill out the reservations form with information you hear. Listen several times if necessary.

	Skyview Suites Reservations	
Address: @ http://skyviewsuites		› go

Skyview Suites Conference Center   *Reservations*

Date of booking   August 15
Arrival date [   ]   Departure date [   ]

Occupancy [select one]   ○ 1 person   ○ 2 persons   ○ more
Room type [select one]   ○ single   ○ double   ○ suite
Beds [select one]   ○ king   ○ queen   ○ two queens

Traveler contact information
Name   Adam Stern
Address   10 Bank Street
          White Lanes, LA 70822

Payment information
Credit card [select one]   ○ USExpress   ○ MultiCard   ○ Wild Card
Card number [   ]   Expiration date [   ]   Agent [Melanie]
Reservation number [   ]

➤ Do it yourself!

Role play. Choose the name of a hotel from the phone book or from a travel ad in the newspaper. Then make reservations for a stay.

Hotel guest: Use the hotel room features from the vocabulary.

Reservations clerk: Use some of these questions plus some of your own questions.

What's your arrival date?

- What's your departure date?
- What type of accommodations do you need?
- Will you be traveling alone?
- Would you prefer a king-size bed or two queens?
- Would you like to guarantee that for late arrival?
- Credit card number? And the expiration date?
- Is the card in your name?

🎧 Vocabulary

Hotel room features

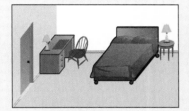

a single room

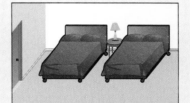

a double room

a suite

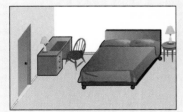

a king-size bed *or* a king

two queen-size beds *or* two queens

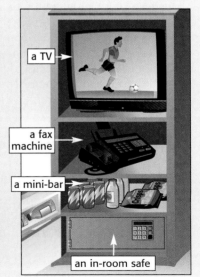

a TV

a fax machine

a mini-bar

an in-room safe

a rollaway bed

a data port

Vacations

A. Read and listen to the letters.

Ask Joan

Culture tips for newcomers

Dear Joan:
I have been working as a medical biller at a large HMO, and I get two weeks of vacation after one year. Joan, this is a *paid* vacation! I feel so lucky. I would like to plan a wonderful driving trip for my family. My family has been in this country for three years, and this is the first time we will be taking a real vacation away from the city! We'd like to see something beautiful in our new country. Any suggestions?
Edward from Bedford

Dear Edward:
Congratulations on your upcoming anniversary! You don't give me much information about your budget, your family's tastes, or how far you want to go. So here are three rules for a good vacation.
- Plan ahead: If you will be staying in a hotel or a motel, it's a good idea to make reservations. There's

nothing worse than not finding a place to sleep after a long day driving or enjoying the outdoors.
- Be cash smart: Carry traveler's checks, credit cards, or an ATM card. It's not a good idea to carry around a lot of cash. Better safe than sorry.
- Shop around: If you have Internet access, surf the travel sites for bargains and package deals. It's possible to save a lot of money on rental cars, plane fares, and hotels if you book in advance and are willing to be flexible about travel dates and times.

Have fun. There's a beautiful country out there to see, wonderful sights, and friendly people.
Joan

Dear Joan:
Last week I got a phone call telling me that I had won a free vacation!!! All I have to do is choose one of three holiday packages and overnight a deposit in cash. Then the company will send me the tickets. The airfare and the taxis are free. The only thing I have to pay for is the hotel. But I have to hurry,

because the offer is good for only one week. Joan, you know this country, so my question to you is this: Which would be the best package—"Aloha, Hawaii," "Star-Studded Hollywood," or "Hot Salsa New York"? Please answer soon!
Gullible Gus

Dear Gullible:
WHOA! Slow down. That free vacation offer sounds too good to be true. And you know when something sounds too good to be true, it usually is. While some package deals are legitimate, don't fall for one that claims to be free. Pressuring you to send cash is also a red flag. More and more readers are writing to me about travel scams that turned their travel dreams into travel nightmares. So, before you send any money, get the details and any refund policy in writing so you can be sure you know what the final costs really might be.

There's an old American saying: "There's no such thing as a free lunch."
Joan

B. Choose an answer to each question. Fill in the ovals.

1. How can you save money on a vacation?
   - ⓐ plan ahead and shop around
   - ⓑ send cash

2. How can a traveler be cash smart?
   - ⓐ carry enough cash to pay for all expenses
   - ⓑ use traveler's checks, credit cards, and ATM cards

3. Where can you find good deals and discounted tickets?
   - ⓐ on the Internet
   - ⓑ in star-studded Hollywood

C. Read the information about travel fraud from the FTC Web site.

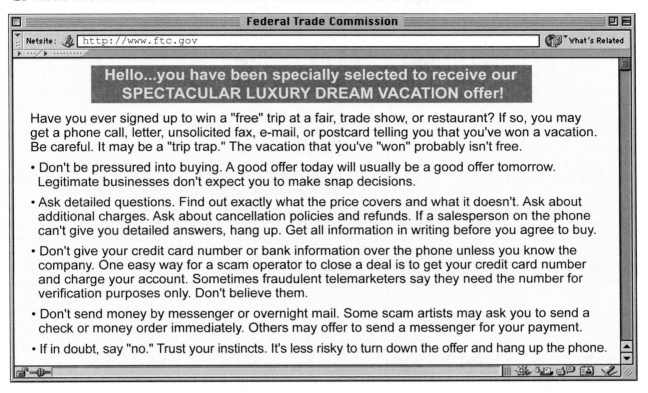

Federal Trade Commission

Netsite: http://www.ftc.gov · What's Related

Hello...you have been specially selected to receive our SPECTACULAR LUXURY DREAM VACATION offer!

Have you ever signed up to win a "free" trip at a fair, trade show, or restaurant? If so, you may get a phone call, letter, unsolicited fax, e-mail, or postcard telling you that you've won a vacation. Be careful. It may be a "trip trap." The vacation that you've "won" probably isn't free.

- Don't be pressured into buying. A good offer today will usually be a good offer tomorrow. Legitimate businesses don't expect you to make snap decisions.

- Ask detailed questions. Find out exactly what the price covers and what it doesn't. Ask about additional charges. Ask about cancellation policies and refunds. If a salesperson on the phone can't give you detailed answers, hang up. Get all information in writing before you agree to buy.

- Don't give your credit card number or bank information over the phone unless you know the company. One easy way for a scam operator to close a deal is to get your credit card number and charge your account. Sometimes fraudulent telemarketers say they need the number for verification purposes only. Don't believe them.

- Don't send money by messenger or overnight mail. Some scam artists may ask you to send a check or money order immediately. Others may offer to send a messenger for your payment.

- If in doubt, say "no." Trust your instincts. It's less risky to turn down the offer and hang up the phone.

D. Warn this consumer about travel fraud. Then compare warnings with your classmates.

Congratulations! A space has been reserved for you at the romantic "San Juan for Lovers" timeshare extravaganza excursion. All inclusive. Very exclusive. To claim your prize, call 1-800-SANJUAN. But hurry! Time is limited.

_____

_____

_____

_____

➤ Do it yourself!

A. True story. Tell a true vacation or travel story. Choose one of these topics:

- your best vacation
- your worst vacation
- the vacation you would like to take

Include information about transportation, accommodations, and travel companions.

B. Culture talk. Is your home country a travel destination for foreign tourists? What are some things tourists there should be careful of? Compare information.

🎧 **B.** **Listening comprehension. Listen to the conversation. Then answer the questions.**

1. Where are the husband and wife? _____

   _____

2. Who does the husband call on the telephone? _____

   _____

🎧 **C.** **Listen again and check the items on the room service order slip.**

Fawlty Suites

Room Service Order Slip   Room No. _____   Time _____

☑ shrimp cocktail   ☐ small   ☐ jumbo

soup   ☐ consomme   ☐ tomato bisque

☐ sirloin steak   ☐ rare   ☐ medium   ☐ well done

☐ chicken   ☐ fried   ☐ broiled   ☐ barbecued

vegetables   ☐ broccoli   ☐ corn

salad dressing   ☐ Italian   ☐ Ranch   ☐ Thousand Island   ☐ French

D. **Read each sentence or question. Underline your response.**

1. "I asked the bellman to pick up my luggage, but he never came."

   YOU Please accept my apology.   **YOU** Will you be traveling alone?

2. "Would you like to guarantee that reservation for late arrival?"

   YOU No, thanks. I travel cash smart.   **YOU** Sure. What do you need—a credit card?

3. "When will you be checking in?"

   YOU I'd prefer to charge that on this card.   **YOU** Pretty late. Maybe I'd better guarantee the room.

4. "Can I make an imprint of your card?"

   YOU Of course. Here you go.   **YOU** I never give my card number over the phone.

E. Complete each statement with *some* or *any*.

1. We don't have _____ bellmen available right now.

2. The guest in Room 566 ordered _____ audiovisual equipment for a meeting.

3. This hotel doesn't have _____ room service. Let's go out.

4. We have _____ nice doubles facing the ocean.

5. There isn't _____ noise from the street.

F. Choose one of the words or phrases to complete each sentence.

1. If you have a lot of cash or valuables, you should request _____.
   a mini-bar / an in-room safe

2. Mr. Martin is traveling with his wife and son. He reserved a double room and a _____.
   rollaway bed / data port

3. They have some memos to send, so they need a room with a _____.
   fax machine / suite

4. Ms. Thompson is on a business trip and needs to check her e-mail. She reserved a room with _____.
   a data port / two queens

G. Composition. **On a separate sheet of paper, write about the picture on page 54. Say as much as you can.**

> **Now I can**
> ☐ request service and respond to requests for service.
> ☐ make and respond to complaints about bad service.
> ☐ make and guarantee hotel reservations.
> ☐ check in at a hotel.
> ☐ evaluate offers for vacation packages.
> ☐ protect myself against travel fraud.

Time

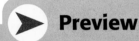 **Preview**

Warm up. What do these documents have in common?

```
GREEN GABLES PUBLIC LIBRARY
        8/30/2004
        05:28 PM

GREEN GABLES PUBLIC LIBRARY
TO RENEW, REQUEST, OR RESERVE
Call 696-4212 during business hours

Mon., Wed., Fri. 1 - 5:30
Tues., Thurs. 10 - 8; Sat. 10 - 5:30

Title: The night of the hunter
Author: Grubb, Davis
Item ID: 0011400823826
Due: 09/13/2004
```

FLORIDA
DRIVER LICENSE
ID: 215 776 536
DOB: 03-08-44
MANNERS, JOAN
87 CROSS CREEK RD
COCONUT CITY, FL 33146
SEX: F EYES: BL HT: 5-05 CLASS: D
ISSUED: 7-16-02 EXPIRES: 03-08-10
Joan Manners
05205844

To Make Application to Register to Vote, You Must:

- Be **a citizen of the United States** for at least one month before the next election;
- Be **a resident of Pennsylvania** and your election district for at least 30 days before the next election; and
- Be **at least 18 years of age** on the day of the next election.

Do you meet these qualifications?

Unit 5 objectives

- Understand the consequences of missing deadlines.
- Apologize for missing an appointment.
- Manage time.
- Prioritize.
- Anticipate and plan actions necessary to make deadlines.

Practical conversations

A. Listen and read.

A: Oh, no. I don't believe it!

B: What?

A: I was supposed to return these books by the 14th. I'll have to pay a fine.

B: Can I give you some advice?

A: Sure. What?

B: Write everything down. That way you won't forget.

B. Pronunciation and intonation practice.

Vocabulary

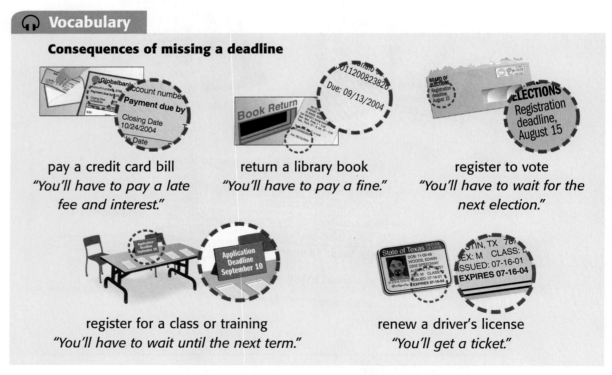

Consequences of missing a deadline

pay a credit card bill
"You'll have to pay a late fee and interest."

return a library book
"You'll have to pay a fine."

register to vote
"You'll have to wait for the next election."

register for a class or training
"You'll have to wait until the next term."

renew a driver's license
"You'll get a ticket."

C. Pair work. Express dismay. Offer advice.

A: Oh, no. I don't believe it!

B: _____?

A: I was supposed to _____. I'll _____.

B: Can I give you some advice?

A: _____?

B: Write everything down. That way you won't forget.

A. Listen and read.

A: Hello?

B: Mrs. Martin? This is Paula in Dr. Paine's office. You had a 2:00 appointment.

A: Oh, no! You're right! I missed it.

B: Would you like to reschedule?

A: Yes, I would. I'm so sorry.

B. Pronunciation and intonation practice.

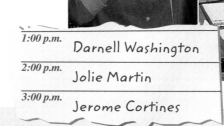

1:00 p.m.   Darnell Washington

2:00 p.m.   Jolie Martin

3:00 p.m.   Jerome Cortines

Vocabulary

Appointments

a doctor's appointment

a dentist's appointment

an orthodontist's appointment

a car service appointment

a hairdresser's appointment

a music lesson

C. Pair work. Apologize for missing an appointment. Use one of the appointments above or your own appointment.

A: Hello?

B: _____? This is _____. You had a _____.

A: Oh, no! You're right! I missed it.

B: Would you like to reschedule?

A: _____.

➤ Do it yourself!

A. Write your appointments, deadlines, and other plans for the next week in this chart.

Appointment or deadline	Consequence of missing it
Monday: *car service appointment*	*The car won't pass inspection.*
Monday:	
Tuesday:	
Wednesday:	
Thursday:	
Friday:	

B. Discussion. Tell your classmates about an appointment you missed in the past. What was the reason? What was the consequence?

Practical grammar

Conditional sentences

Use *if* in conditional sentences for both real and unreal conditions.

Real conditions (facts)

             if clause   result clause

    If you miss an appointment, you have to reschedule.

    If I miss one more appointment, I'll have to pay.

Unreal conditions

    If she knew the number, she would call. (unreal: She doesn't know it.)

A. **Read the conditional sentences. Check the ones that describe an unreal condition.**

1. ☐ If you return a library book after the due date, you have to pay a fine.

2. ☐ If Carl took music lessons, he would be a better pianist.

3. ☐ If your teeth are crooked, the orthodontist can straighten them.

4. ☐ If you don't register before the deadline, you won't be able to vote.

5. ☐ If my mother doesn't wear her glasses, she's not allowed to drive.

6. ☐ If I were you, I'd write everything down.

7. ☐ If they registered for the class today, they would get a discount.

8. ☐ If we always paid on time, we wouldn't have to pay a late fee.

Verb forms in conditional sentences

Real conditions

Use *if* and the simple present tense in the *if* clause, even if the result is in the future.

             if clause   result clause

    If I **return** this book late, I'll pay the fine.

Don't use a future form (*will, be going to*) in the *if* clause.

    ~~If I will return this book late, I'll pay the fine.~~

Unreal conditions

Use *if* and the simple past tense or *were* to state an unreal condition. Use *would* or *could* and a verb in the result clause. *Could* is less certain than *would*.

    If Paul **wore** his glasses, he **could see** better. (unreal: He doesn't wear them.)

    If I **were** in your shoes, I**'d return** that book on time.

    If she **were** a doctor, she**'d be** a pediatrician.

Don't use *would* or *could* in the *if* clause.

    ~~If she would be a doctor, she would be a pediatrician.~~

> In all conditional sentences, the clauses can be reversed with no change in meaning.
>
> If you don't return the book on time, you'll pay a fine.
>
> You'll pay a fine if you don't return the book on time.

B. First complete each conditional sentence as a real condition. Then write the sentence as an unreal condition.

1. He ___will go___ back to school if he ___has___ enough time.
      go   have
   He would go back to school if he had enough time.

2. If I _____ my electronics certification, I _____ a better job.
        get   get

   _____

3. If the library _____ open this afternoon, I _____ these books.
                   be   return

   _____

4. If she _____ the deadline, she _____ in this election.
           miss   not vote

   _____

5. _____ you _____ for English classes at work if they _____ offered?
                register   be

   _____

➤ Do it yourself!

A. Write what you would or could do if you had more time and more money.

If I had more time,	If I had more money,
I could learn to play the guitar.	_I would take a great vacation._

B. Collaborative activity. Write all your sentences on the board in two lists. Then compare with your group or class.

Authentic practice

A. Read the picture story again. Answer the questions.

1. Why is Mrs. Gebert apologizing? _____

2. Why is Mrs. Gebert having a problem? _____

3. What advice does Ms. Fun give her? _____

B. Vocabulary. Choose one of the words or phrases in the box to complete each sentence.

make ends meet	better late than never	juggle
total overload	no picnic	

1. Many people have to _____ parenthood and career. It's a time management problem.

2. When a mother or a father goes back to school, it's hard to _____ if the other parent doesn't work.

3. When you have too many commitments, you feel like you're on _____.

4. Start organizing your day beginning right now: _____.

5. Another way to say something is really hard is "It's _____."

🎧 **C.** Listen. Read each response out loud from the text on page 62.

D. Read each sentence or question. Underline your response.

1. "Please accept my apology."

   YOU Don't worry. It's OK.　　　YOU I don't believe it!

2. "Why did you miss the appointment?"

   YOU I just couldn't make ends meet.　　YOU I just have too much on my plate.

3. "It's really hard to make ends meet."

   YOU You're working right now, aren't you?　　YOU Thank goodness.

4. "I'm on total overload!"

   YOU Better late than never.　　YOU I know—it's no picnic.

5. "What would you do if you were in my shoes?"

   YOU I'd ask my mother to help.　　YOU That's good advice.

E. Pair work. Take turns reading the items and responses in Exercise D.

➤ Do it yourself!

A. Write your own response. Then read each conversation out loud with a partner.

> You look like you're on total overload. What's the matter?

YOU _____

> What are you going to do to avoid missing so many appointments?

YOU _____

> If you don't mind my advice, I think you should make a list. That way you'll remember everything.

YOU _____

B. Culture talk. In the country you come from, is juggling family and work more complicated or less complicated than it is here? Compare cultures with your classmates.

Authentic practice

Time management

A. Listening comprehension. Listen to the lecture on time management. Then listen again. As you listen, take notes on what Dr. Gutentag says.

> NOTES
> _____
> _____
> _____
> _____

B. Discussion. Answer the question. Then discuss with a partner.

According to the lecture, what can we do to help manage our time? _____

_____

C. Vocabulary. Choose one of the words from the box to complete each sentence.

perfectionism	procrastination	prioritization

1. Doing the most important things before doing the least important things is

   _____.

2. Putting off until tomorrow what you can do today is _____.

3. Expecting yourself to do everything well is _____.

D. Read about Ramon Cruz's and Wendy Del Aguila's time management problems. Then choose advice from the list below or give your own advice.

> Ask someone else to help.
> Reschedule a less important commitment.
> Prioritize—you've got too much on your plate.
> Just say no.

1. Ramon Cruz works from 9:00 to 5:00. His wife just had foot surgery. She can't walk or drive for a week. His daughter has a doctor's appointment on Tuesday at 4:00. His son has soccer practice at 3:30 on Tuesday and Thursday. His wife agreed to help at voter registration on Wednesday, and they have books due at the library.

   Your advice to Ramon Cruz: _____

64   Unit 5

2. Wendy Del Aguila bit off more than she can chew. She's a Girl Scout den mother, a volunteer at the hospital, the mother of three children, and a single parent. Wendy works until 3:00 in the office of her children's school and then carpools three days a week. On Tuesday, Wendy hears about a Girl Scout bake sale. She'd like to bake cookies with the girls in her kitchen on Wednesday, but her driver's license will expire on Thursday.

Your advice to Wendy Del Aguila: _____

E. **Discussion. Describe the consequences of missing each deadline in Exercise D. Use *if*.**

If he doesn't return the library books, he'll have to pay a fine.

➤ Do it yourself!

A. **Make your own "to-do" list for tomorrow or for this week.**

To do!
_____
_____
_____
_____

B. **Prioritize your list.**

- A for things you have to do no matter what
- B for things you'll do if you have the time
- C for things you don't really have to do or that you can get someone else to do

C. **Discussion. Discuss your list and your priorities with a partner or a group.**

If I don't do the laundry today, the kids won't have anything to wear!

If I don't buy groceries today, I could buy them tomorrow.

The importance of time sensitivity

🎧 **A.** Read and listen to the letters.

Ask Joan
Culture tips for newcomers

Dear Joan:

I just can't get used to one thing in this country. I think people here are very nervous about time. And they are making me nervous too!

At work I have to punch a time clock, and if I'm five minutes late from my break, my manager gives me a dirty look. If I come late to someone's house for a party, they are unfriendly to me.

I think this is silly, and I think people should just relax! What would happen if someone brought a book back to the library a couple of days late? What would the big deal be? Sometimes it takes a little longer to finish the book. And if the people who are giving the party are my friends, why do they mind if I'm not right on time? And what's so terrible if I pay my rent a day or two late? The landlord has a lot of money. Believe me, he won't starve!

Please explain to me, Joan: Why are the people here so crazy about schedules and time? I think it's very unfriendly.

Deborah in Dallas

Dear Deborah:

You don't say where you come from, but it is true that each culture has its own ideas about the importance of schedules, times, and dates. Adjusting to a different concept of time can be very difficult, even more difficult than adjusting to other customs such as food or clothing styles.

It's very hard to explain why one culture has one idea and another culture sees things differently. In every culture, though, "rules" have developed in order to prevent conflicts and misunderstandings between people.

If you think about this a little, you will realize that in some ways time is important to you too. I'm sure you don't like to wait a long time when you have an appointment to see a doctor or a dentist. Remember, Deborah, that no matter how different our cultures may seem, people all over the world are basically the same: friendly, fun-loving, hardworking, but in ways that may look different from the outside.

Joan

B. **Culture talk.** Discuss the following questions.

1. What do you think about the attitudes toward time in this country? Do they make you uncomfortable? Have you adjusted? Give examples.

2. If someone from this culture went to live in your country, what cultural rules would be difficult to understand or adjust to? Give examples so your classmates will understand.

3. Where do you think Deborah comes from originally? Why do you think that?

C. **Collaborative activity. With a group, make a list of things to do and documents to prepare to register a child named Grace Lukin for kindergarten in September. Decide together when to do each activity. Today's date is April 1.**

- Grace has no family doctor.
- She needs a polio booster.
- Her fifth birthday is September 10.
- She lives in the Grafton School attendance area.

Denton Area City Schools

Kindergarten Registration

Denton Area City Schools will hold kindergarten registration during the week of May 6 through May 9. Each elementary school building will register students in its attendance area as follows:

Monday, May 6	Tuesday, May 7	Wednesday, May 8	Thursday, May 9
Smith School	Grafton School	Denton School	Ennis School
(426-0572)	(265-5372)	(466-0224)	(486-0705)

Students whose last names begin with A through L will register between 8:30 and 11:30 a.m., while M through Z will register between 12:30 and 3:30 p.m.

Registration packets will be available at each elementary school office after April 8. Parents are asked to pick up and complete the registration forms prior to registration day.

To be eligible for kindergarten, students must be five years old by September 30. Children whose birthday falls after September 30 will not enter kindergarten until the following year.

PLEASE BRING YOUR CHILD, and the following information, as required by law, with you for registration:
1. Birth Certificate
2. Social Security Number
3. Registration Form
4. Written Proof of Immunization:
   * DPT (diphtheria, pertussis, tetanus) — minimum of 4 (including 1 booster)
   * Polio — minimum of 3 or 4 (including 1 booster)
   * MMR (measles, mumps, rubella) — 2 doses of each
   * Hepatitis B — 3 doses
5. Proof of Legal Guardianship

If you do not have a family doctor to complete the necessary immunizations, the Clark County Health Department sponsors the following clinics:
   * Every Tuesday, 10:00 a.m. – 12:00 noon, Denton Community Center
   * Every Monday and Friday, 9:00 a.m. – 3:00 p.m., Denton Health Department

D. **Discussion. Write your lists on the board and compare.**

➤ Do it yourself!   A plan-ahead project

Choose one of these subjects and get information about deadlines. Compare information with your classmates. Make a "to-do" list.

- registering a child at a day-care center
- voter registration
- community college registration
- immunizations for schoolchildren

B. Listening comprehension. Read the document. Then listen to the conversation.

> If you are under the age of 18 and hold a junior driver's license, you can bring proof of completion of a driver education course approved by the

C. Read the statements and listen to the conversation again. Then check *True* or *False* for each statement.

	True	False
1. The caller wants to renew her daughter's driver's license.	☐	☐
2. The girl will be sixteen in June.	☐	☐
3. You can only take driver's ed at your own high school.	☐	☐
4. If you are seventeen, you have to take driver's ed to get a senior license.	☐	☐

D. Read each sentence or question. Underline your response.

1. "Do you mind if I give you a tip?"

   YOU How much?   **YOU** Not at all.

2. "What would you do if you were in my shoes?"

   YOU I'd prioritize.   **YOU** I'd procrastinate.

3. "It sounds like you're on total overload."

   YOU Yes. I've got too much on my plate.   **YOU** Better late than never.

4. "What would you do if you couldn't make ends meet?"

   YOU I would have no choice.   **YOU** I'd get a night job.

E. Read the conditional sentences. Check the ones that describe an unreal condition.

1. ☐ If you take driver's ed, you can get a license earlier.
2. ☐ If Pete got some more training, he could get a promotion.
3. ☐ If I worked a second job, I could make ends meet.
4. ☐ If you don't have three DPT shots, you can't register for kindergarten.

F. Complete each real conditional sentence with a result clause.

1. If you pay a credit card bill after the due date, _____.

2. If you have an overdue library book, _____.

3. If you forget to renew your driver's license, _____.

4. If you don't register to vote, _____.

G. Complete each unreal conditional sentence with the correct form of the verb.

1. He _____ driver's ed if he _____ in a hurry to get a license.
        take   be

2. If I _____ back to school, I _____ a part-time job.
         go   need

3. If the DMV _____ open on weekends, I _____ my driver's test sooner.
           be   take

4. What do you think he _____ if he _____ in your shoes?
             do   be

H. Read the overdue policy from the Milwaukee, Wisconsin, public library system. Then compute the overdue charges on this book. Today's date is June 1.

Charges: _____

TITLE: **Overload! It's not the end of the world.**
DUE: 03/15

Milwaukee Public Library

Address: @ http://www.mpl.org/File/libcard_about.htm   › go

Overdue charges

- The fee is 10 cents per item per day, including Sundays and holidays. For most items there is a three-day grace period during which no fines are charged. On the fourth day the overdue charges total 40 cents.
- The maximum overdue charge is $5 per item.
- There are no fines on overdue materials checked out on children's library cards, except videos, DVDs and puppets.
- Rental books may be checked out for $1 per week. When rental books are not returned in one week, cardholders are charged $1 for each additional week (or portion of a week) the books are out.
- The Milwaukee Public Library accepts Master Card and Visa.

Web zone

I. **Composition.** On a separate sheet of paper, write about the picture on page 68. Say as much as you can.

> **Now I can**
> ❑ understand the consequences of missing deadlines.
> ❑ apologize for missing an appointment.
> ❑ manage time.
> ❑ prioritize.
> ❑ anticipate and plan actions necessary to make deadlines.

Supplies and services

> **Preview**

Warm up. What is the purpose of an estimate? Which painter would you hire? Why?

Velela Household Painting
15678 E. Dakota Avenue, Denver, CO 80232
(303) 555-7838

Mr. and Mrs. Paul Mitchell
45 Plainview Court, Milton, CO 80231
Paint all sides of house with Silas Morton paints, 2 coats
Estimate: $4,500, including labor and supplies

KBS **Konstantanides Building Services**
4597 Brenner Avenue, Milton, CO 80211

For Paul Mitchell, 45 Plainview Court
Paint house, 2 coats, $3,600 + labor

Unit 6 objectives

- Ask for a recommendation of a person who provides a service.
- Ask for an estimate and get it in writing.
- Make an agreement.
- Understand homeowner's, car, and life insurance.

Practical conversations

A. Listen and read.

> A: Can you give me an estimate?
> B: Yes. It'll be about $500.
> A: How long will it take?
> B: Three or four days.
> A: Will you put that in writing?
> B: Of course. No problem.

B. Pronunciation and intonation practice.

Vocabulary

Services you should get an estimate for

a paint job

dental work

an auto repair

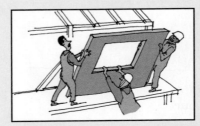

construction

plumbing

electrical work

C. Pair work. Ask for an estimate. Get it in writing.

> A: Can you give me an estimate?
> B: _____. It'll be about $_____.
> A: How long will it take?
> B: _____.
> A: Will you put that in writing?
> B: _____.

A. Listen and read.

A: Do you know a good painter?

B: As a matter of fact, I do. Would you like me to give you his name?

A: Is he reasonable?

B: Yes. And he does a really good job.

A: Thanks. That sounds like a good reference!

B. Pronunciation and intonation practice.

Vocabulary

Descriptions of good workers

reasonable: doesn't charge too much

fast: completes the job quickly

honest: is truthful and meets commitments

efficient: doesn't waste time

reliable: delivers on promises

C. Pair work. Ask for a recommendation. Use the people in the box or your own service people.

painter	dentist	hairdresser	babysitter
mover	doctor	plumber	electrician

A: Do you know a good _____?

B: As a matter of fact, I do. Would you like me to give you _____ name?

A: Is _____ _____?

B: Yes. And _____ does a really good job.

A: _____. That sounds like a good reference!

➤ Do it yourself!

True story. Recommend a service provider you have used and explain why. Or describe a bad experience you have had with a service provider.

Type of service	Recommendation or problem
painting: *Powell Company*	*Pete is reliable and does good work.*
plumbing: *Pincus Pipes*	*The workers left a mess and were late.*

Practical grammar

The sentence: Definition

A sentence is a group of words with a subject and a verb that expresses a complete idea.

subject   verb

The Johnsons know a good painter.

A. Check the groups of words that are sentences.

1. ☐ Four old houses.

2. ☐ The insurance policy is.

3. ☐ The insurance policy is paid.

4. ☐ They called the FTC to make a complaint.

5. ☐ Seven houses in the neighborhood but no more than eight.

6. ☐ They volunteered.

7. ☐ The painter said he would finish in a week.

8. ☐ We didn't volunteer.

9. ☐ He's an aggressive driver.

10. ☐ She's great.

11. ☐ An estimate.

B. Pair work. Explain your answers in Exercise A.

"Four old houses" has no verb.

"The insurance policy is" is not a complete thought.

The sentence: Punctuation and capitalization

Always capitalize the first word of a sentence. Always use a period or a question mark at the end.

She's the president of the insurance company.

Is he a claims adjuster?

C. Rewrite the sentences and questions with correct capitalization and punctuation.

1. where is the exit _____

2. whose policy is this _____

3. is Mr. Sutherland here _____

4. there's something wrong with it _____

5. it's hard to know all the terms _____

D. **Pair work.** **Explain your punctuation and capitalization decisions in Exercise C.**

Other capitalization rules

Capitalize the first letter of a person's names.
　　Roberto Lopez
Capitalize the first letter of titles: *Mr., Ms., Mrs., Miss, Dr.* (Don't capitalize the word *doctor* unless it's a title.)
　　Dr. Roberts can see you now.　　　　　She's a doctor.
Capitalize the first letter of names of streets, cities, states, and countries.
When you write an address, use a comma between the city and the state.

Solange Phillips
6301 Victoria Pl.
Perry, NY 10514

Dr. Caroline Svesko
99 Main Street
Perry, NY 10514

E. **Write your name and address.**

Name: _____

Address: _____

F. **Rewrite the sentences and questions with correct capitalization and punctuation.**

1. ms laura brown lives in chicago _____

2. the address is 78 haights cross road _____

3. mr mitchell asked two companies to give him an estimate _____

　　_____

4. were they born in peru _____

5. when did you move to casper wyoming _____

　　_____

➤ Do it yourself!　　　A do-ahead project

Bring an envelope to class. Find the name of a plumber, a painter, or another service provider (such as a doctor, dentist, lawyer) in the Yellow Pages. Address an envelope to him or her. Include your return address (your own name and address) on the envelope.

Make an insurance claim

A. Discussion. Answer the questions in your own words. Then discuss with your group.

1. What happened? _____

2. Why is the woman talking to the man? _____

3. What does he want to know? _____

4. What advice does she give him? _____

B. Check the subjects the homeowner and the insurance adjuster talk about. Listen again if necessary.

1. ☐ painting   4. ☐ storm damage

2. ☐ contacting the police   5. ☐ insurance coverage

3. ☐ tree removal

C. Vocabulary. **Choose one of the words or phrases to complete each sentence.**

1. A _____ is a written agreement with an insurance company.
   policy / removal

2. Insurance doesn't _____ all costs of the policyholder.
   damage / cover

3. Another way to say "covered" is _____.
   insured / claimed

4. The _____ describe who is responsible for repairing damage.
   terms / words of mouth

5. Another way to say "an estimate" is a _____.
   quote / deal

D. Read each sentence or question. **Underline your response.**

1. "Do you know the terms of the policy?"

   YOU As a matter of fact, I don't.   **YOU** I think you should ask around.

2. "How much will it cost?"

   YOU We've run out of money.   **YOU** It can run into a lot of money.

3. "This is some policy. It doesn't cover anything!"

   YOU You can thank your lucky stars.   **YOU** You can say that again.

4. "Do you know how to get the best deal?"

   YOU Check the policy.   **YOU** Get more than one quote.

E. Pair work. **Take turns reading the items and responses in Exercise D.**

➤ Do it yourself!

A. Write your own response. **Then read each conversation out loud with a partner.**

What a mess! Can you recommend someone to help me clean this up?   **YOU** _____

I had fire damage in my kitchen, and I need to make a claim. Do you know what's covered?   **YOU** _____

Look at that house. That was some fire!   **YOU** _____

B. Culture talk. **In the country you come from, do people have insurance? What kinds? Compare cultures with your classmates.**

Authentic practice

Competitive bids for service

🎧 **A.** **Listening comprehension. Listen to the conversations.**

Speedy Tree Removal
Fast service...Honest estimates
914-555-6200

The Chapman Chipmunk
860-555-2111
All kinds of tree service.

🎧 **B.** **Listen to the conversations again. Complete the chart.**

Speedy Tree Removal	The Chapman Chipmunk
can start: *tomorrow*	can start:
price:	price:
will finish:	will finish:

🎧 **C.** **Discussion. Talk about these questions with your classmates. Listen again if necessary.**

- What happened?
- What does Mr. Adams want?
- Which company got the job?
- Why?

D. **Role play. Mr. Adams's tree was removed. Now he has to repair the roof, paint the house, and replace the fence that was destroyed by the tree. All the repairs are covered by his homeowner's insurance policy.**

Read the questions Mr. Adams asked the contractors. Then role-play conversations between Mr. Adams and a roofer, a painter, and a person who builds fences. Fill in the estimates on page 79.

So you say $___, plus $___ for tips? Day and a half?

Can you put that all in writing?

When could you start?

So, you think you'll be finished by ___?

TIP TOP
ROOFING
102 Shanley Avenue
Newark, NJ 07045
Estimate

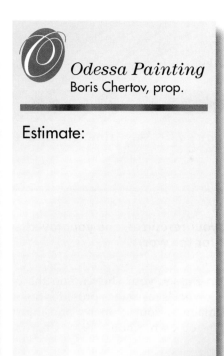

Odessa Painting
Boris Chertov, prop.

Estimate:

UNIVERSAL FENCE
149 Tillson Lake Road
Gardiner, NJ 07079

➤ Do it yourself!

A. True story. **Did you ever have damage to your house or apartment? Or have you read about such damage? What happened? What was the cause? Complete the chart.**

Damage	Date	Cause
broken windows	May 19, 2001	earthquake

B. Discussion. **Tell the class your story.**

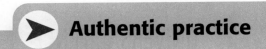

Authentic practice

A. Read about insurance in *Today's Life* Magazine. Then take the insurance self-test.

Today's Life Magazine   November 2004   **41**

Insurance Basics
**How to protect your property, your resources, and your loved ones
Hope for the best. . . BUT plan for the worst**

Homeowner's Insurance
Your home is your most expensive asset, your shelter, and the place you keep your belongings. Homeowner's insurance provides financial protection against disasters—damage to your property and injury to other people or their property. If you own a house or an apartment, you need it.

Auto Insurance
Auto insurance protects you against financial loss if you have an accident. It generally covers damage to or loss of your car and injury or property damage to others. Most states require you to carry some car insurance coverage.

Life Insurance
Life insurance pays your beneficiaries in case of your death. If other people depend on your income, then you need life insurance. Life insurance helps pay short-term expenses, such as funeral costs, medical bills, debt, and taxes, and long-term expenses, such as college expenses, mortgage payments, etc.

Health Insurance
Health insurance coverage comes in many forms and combinations. One form is a health maintenance organization, or HMO. Some policies pay all or part of your medical costs, doctor's bills, and prescription drug costs. See next month's issue for a complete presentation of the pros and cons of different types of health insurance.

INSURANCE SELF-TEST. Check the statements that are true for you.

☐ I need homeowner's insurance.   ☐ I need life insurance.

☐ I need auto insurance.   ☐ I need health insurance.

Key Insurance Terms

insurance A contract between you and an insurance company to make payments to you or another person in case of injury, damage, or death

premium The amount you pay the insurance company for coverage

liability Your legal responsibility to pay the victim of injury or damage you cause either directly or indirectly

beneficiary A person who receives payments from an insurance company

claim A report you make to an insurance company in order to receive payments you are entitled to under the terms of your policy

B. Pair work. Explain your answers in the insurance self-test to a partner.

 FYI. For consumer information about insurance, log on to the following Web sites:

Better Business Bureau
www.bbb.org/bureaus

Coalition Against Insurance Fraud
www.insurancefraud.org

Federal Trade Commission
www.ftc.gov or call (202) 382-4357

Insurance Information Institute
www.iii.org or call (800) 331-9146

C. Read how to prepare the information on an insurance claim after a car accident.

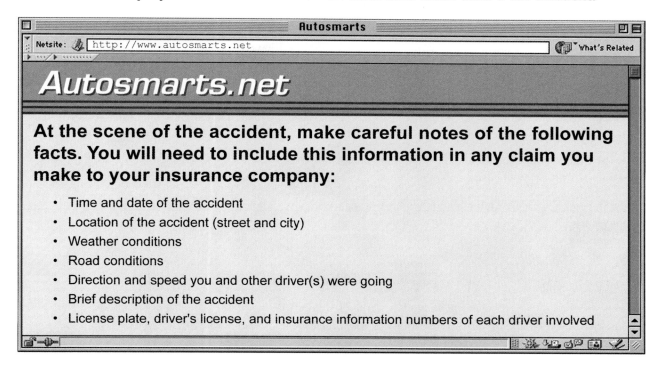

Autosmarts.net

At the scene of the accident, make careful notes of the following facts. You will need to include this information in any claim you make to your insurance company:

- Time and date of the accident
- Location of the accident (street and city)
- Weather conditions
- Road conditions
- Direction and speed you and other driver(s) were going
- Brief description of the accident
- License plate, driver's license, and insurance information numbers of each driver involved

D. Betsy Harris had an accident. Read the notes she took at the scene of the accident.

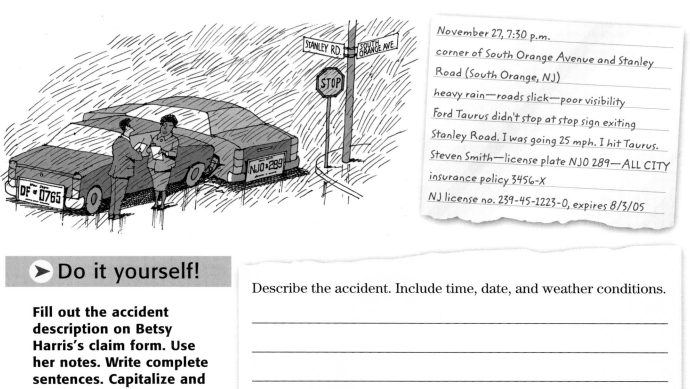

November 27, 7:30 p.m.

corner of South Orange Avenue and Stanley Road (South Orange, NJ)

heavy rain—roads slick—poor visibility

Ford Taurus didn't stop at stop sign exiting Stanley Road. I was going 25 mph. I hit Taurus.

Steven Smith—license plate NJO 289—ALL CITY insurance policy 3456-X

NJ license no. 239-45-1223-0, expires 8/3/05

➤ Do it yourself!

Fill out the accident description on Betsy Harris's claim form. Use her notes. Write complete sentences. Capitalize and punctuate correctly.

Describe the accident. Include time, date, and weather conditions.

_____

_____

_____

_____

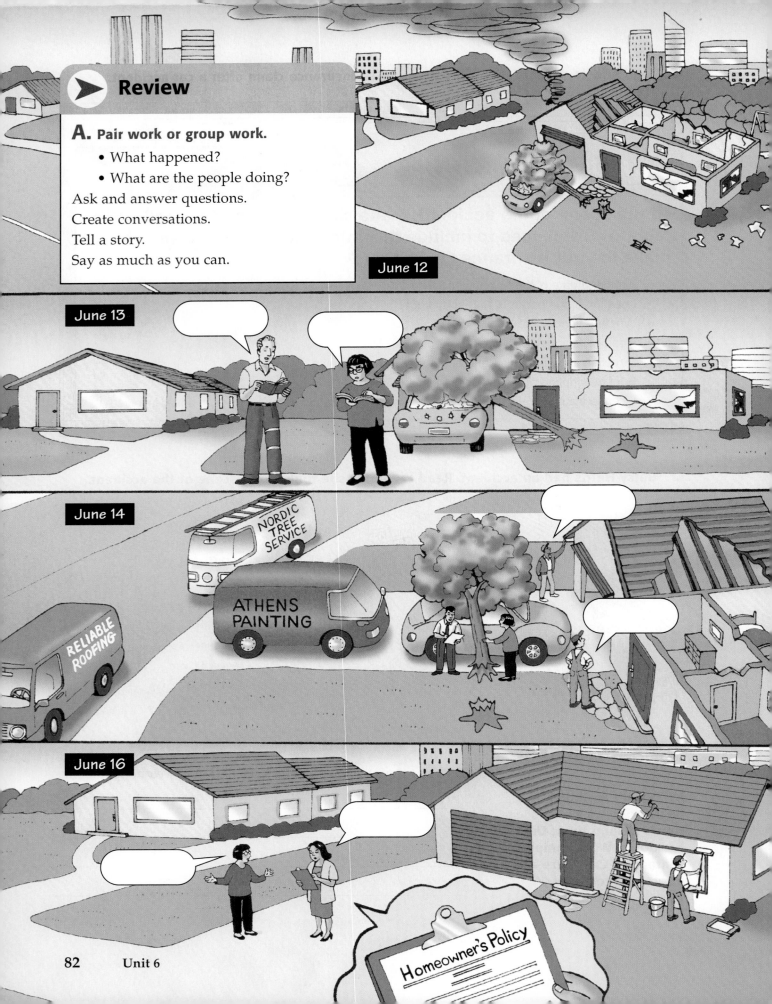

Review

A. Pair work or group work.

- What happened?
- What are the people doing?

Ask and answer questions.

Create conversations.

Tell a story.

Say as much as you can.

1. What happened? _____

2. Why does the woman call her friend Todd after she speaks to the roofers?

   _____

🎧 **C.** Read the statements. Then listen to the conversations again and check *True*, *False*, or *?*
(No information) for each statement.

	True	False	?
1. A tree fell on the roof.	❏	❏	❏
2. No one was hurt.	❏	❏	❏
3. A car caused the damage.	❏	❏	❏
4. The caller got the names of the companies from the Yellow Pages.	❏	❏	❏
5. The caller asked the roofers to put their estimates in writing.	❏	❏	❏

D. Answer the questions.

1. Which roofer did the caller choose, Arbor City or Rubin? _____

2. Why did she make that choice? _____

E. Read each sentence or question. Underline your response.

1. "Can you recommend a good plumber?"

   YOU He's reliable.   **YOU** As a matter of fact, I can.

2. "That sounds like a good reference."

   YOU Personally, no.   **YOU** It is.

3. "That is some mess!"

   YOU You can say that again.   **YOU** Thank you very much.

4. "What's a good way to find a reliable painter?"

   YOU Ask around.   **YOU** That's a relief.

5. "Will you put that in writing?"

   YOU Sure. No problem.   **YOU** That can run into a lot of money.

F. **Choose one of the words or phrases to complete each sentence.**

1. This policy looks great. How much are the _____?
   terms / premiums

2. Before you make a claim, you have to ask for _____.
   an estimate / a deal

3. A worker who doesn't charge too much is _____.
   fast / reasonable

4. Someone who doesn't waste time is _____.
   honest / efficient

5. A worker who does what is promised is _____.
   reasonable / reliable

G. **Rewrite the sentences and questions with the correct capitalization and punctuation.**

1. mr benson is a reliable and efficient painter _____

_____

2. we live at 45 elm street in stony creek _____

_____

3. who wrote this description of the accident in colorado _____

_____

4. ms laura linden is in texas right now _____

_____

H. **Guided composition. Look at the picture on page 82. Complete the story. Use correct capitalization and punctuation.**

On June 12, _____

_____

Then on June 13, _____

_____

Finally, _____

_____

Now I can
- [ ] ask for a recommendation of a person who provides a service.
- [ ] ask for an estimate and get it in writing.
- [ ] make an agreement.
- [ ] understand homeowner's, car, and life insurance.

Relationships

 Preview

Warm up. What do you know about the Constitution of the United States?

THE CONSTITUTION OF THE UNITED STATES

We the People of the United States, in order to form a more perfect union, establish justice, insure domestic tranquility, provide for the common defense, promote the general welfare, and secure the blessings of liberty to ourselves and our posterity, do ordain and establish this Constitution for the United States of America.

Article I

Section 1. All legislative powers herein granted shall be vested in a Congress of the United States, which shall consist of a Senate and House of Representatives.

Amendment I

Congress shall make no law respecting an establishment of religion, or prohibiting the free exercise thereof; or abridging the freedom of speech, or of the press; or the right of the people peaceably to assemble,

Amendment VI

In all criminal prosecutions, the accused shall enjoy the right to a speedy and public trial, by an impartial jury of the state and district wherein the crime shall have been committed, which district shall have been previously

---

Unit 7 objectives

- Discuss pros and cons of controversial issues.
- Agree and disagree respectfully.
- Report what other people say.
- Understand the importance of the U.S. Constitution and the Bill of Rights.
- Understand the elements of the U.S. justice system.

Practical conversations

A. Listen and read.

A: Are you in favor of capital punishment?

B: Yes, I am. I believe in "an eye for an eye." What about you?

A: Actually, I'm against it. I think it's wrong to take a life, no matter what.

B: Well, I guess we'll have to agree to disagree!

B. Pronunciation and intonation practice.

Opinions

I'm in favor of it.   I'm against it.
It's wrong.   It's OK under some circumstances.
It's right.   It's wrong no matter what.

Vocabulary

Sample pros and cons of controversial ideas

Capital punishment
pro I feel that some crimes are so bad that the criminal doesn't have a right to live. If you kill someone, then you should be killed.
con I think it's morally wrong to take a life. If we execute criminals, then we are doing the same thing the criminal did. Also, sometimes innocent people are executed.

Government censorship of books and movies
pro I think some books and movies are too violent and offensive. They can cause crime.
con I don't think government has the right to tell us what we can read or watch.

Organized prayer in public schools
pro I think students would behave better if they prayed in school. Prayer reminds people of what is right and wrong.
con I feel religion is private. Some children are uncomfortable if they are of a different religion or if they have no religion.

C. Pair work. Disagree about a controversial issue. Use an issue above or your own issue.

A: Are you in favor of _____?

B: _____, I _____. What about you?

A: Actually, I'm _____ it. I _____.

B: Well, I guess we'll have to agree to disagree!

A. **Listen and read.**

> **A:** You want to know what I think?
> **B:** What?
> **A:** I think it's ridiculous that you have to wear a seat belt.
> **B:** But seat belts save lives.
> **A:** You have a point. But I just think there are way too many rules.
> **B:** Actually, I agree with that.

B. **Pronunciation and intonation practice.**

Vocabulary

Rules

You have to wear a seat belt / a helmet.

You can't smoke indoors in a public place.

You have to have a license to own a gun.

You can't drink until you're twenty-one, but you can vote and join the Army at eighteen.

Your own rule: _____

C. **Pair work.** **Discuss a rule you don't like.**

> **A:** You want to know what I think?
> **B:** _____?
> **A:** I think it's ridiculous that _____.
> **B:** But _____.
> **A:** You have a point. But _____.
> **B:** Actually, I agree with that.

➤ Do it yourself!

A. **Choose a rule you don't agree with or a controversial issue people disagree about. Then write an argument for and an argument against.**

Issue: _____

   pro _____

   con _____

B. **Discussion.** **Write your opinion on a separate sheet of paper. Begin with "I think" or "I feel." Then discuss.**

Practical grammar

Reporting a person's words: Direct speech

Use quotation marks to write a person's exact words.
    Martin said, "Censorship is wrong."
Put the period or the question mark before the quotation mark at the end of the quoted words.
    Nicole asked, "Why are there so many rules?"

A. **Write quotation marks around the quoted speech.**

1. They asked, Are you in favor of prayer in the schools?

2. We answered, Not in the public schools.

3. Maria said, Actually, I'm for capital punishment under some circumstances.

4. Senator Smith asked, Are you in favor of a constitutional amendment outlawing capital punishment in all circumstances?

5. We said, We'll have to think about that.

B. **Write quotation marks and a period or a question mark at the end of the quoted speech.**

1. Jessica asked, Do you want to know what I think

2. Terry answered, Yes, please tell me

3. Jessica answered, I think it's ridiculous that we have to wear a seat belt

4. Terry said, I do too, but I'm in favor of the law that children have to wear them

5. Jessica responded, To tell you the truth, I agree with that

Use of a comma in quotations

Use a comma after the verb that introduces the quoted speech.
Begin the quoted statement or question with a capital letter.
    The advertisement says, "Seat belts save lives."

C. **Insert a comma and a period or a question mark in each quoted statement and question.**

1. Marcia said "I'm against capital punishment in all circumstances   "

2. Then Paul said "I disagree. I think some crimes are so bad that capital punishment is justified   "

3. She answered "Well, I think it's morally wrong to take a life   "

4. Finally Paul asked "What do you think society should do with terrible criminals   "

5. Marcia answered "Lock them up and throw away the key   "

Sometimes we report a person's speech without using the exact words the person said. This is called indirect speech. Don't use quotation marks for indirect speech. Don't use a comma in indirect speech.

   Paul says, "I disagree with that law." (direct speech)
   Paul says he disagrees with that law. (indirect speech)

Sometimes we use *that* to introduce the indirect speech. There's no change in meaning.

   Paul says **that** he disagrees with that law.

D. **Report what each person says.**

   1. **Adam:** I don't agree.   *Adam says he doesn't agree.*

   2. **Laura:** I'm against censorship.   _____

   3. **Richard:** I'll have to think about it.   _____

   4. **Martina:** I read about that in the paper.   _____

   5. **Mr. Lewis:** Mary has it.   _____

➤ Do it yourself!

A. **Look at the opinion you wrote on page 87. Write that opinion on the board and sign your name.**

B. **On a separate sheet of paper, write your classmates' opinions in direct speech. Then write them in indirect speech.**

Ellen says, "It's silly that you have to be twenty-one to buy cigarettes."

Ellen says that it's silly that you have to be twenty-one to buy cigarettes.

Authentic practice

A mistake about shoplifting

1
That watch is awesome. I'm going to buy it for Mother's Day. What do you think, Paul?

It's beautiful, but $259.... That's out of my price range. I think I'll pass.

It is a little pricey, but I've been saving up for a while . . . in a big piggy bank!

2
That comes to $271.76 with tax. Will that be cash or charge?

Cash, please. Here you go. I have exact change, even the pennies.

Hey, Dan. Later. I'm going to the third floor. I think my mom could use a nice robe for Mother's Day.

3
Could you please tell me where the gift-wrapping department is?

Just my luck. She's gone!

4
Do you have a receipt for that watch, sir?

A. Read the picture story again. Answer the questions.

1. What are Dan and Paul shopping for? _____

2. What does Dan buy? _____

3. Why doesn't Paul buy the same thing for his mom? _____
   _____

4. What does the guard want to see? _____

B. Read each sentence or question. Underline your response.

1. "Do you like this robe?"

   YOU Yes. It's awesome.   **YOU** Actually, I'm against it.

2. "That's out of my price range."

   YOU I have exact change.   **YOU** Mine too. But I've been saving up.

3. "I've got to go now."

   YOU OK. Later.   **YOU** I guess we'll have to agree to disagree.

4. "I'm sorry. There are no more watches."

   YOU I think I'll pass.   **YOU** Just my luck. That's what I wanted.

C. Pair work. Take turns reading the items and responses in Exercise B.

D. Guided composition. Read the story again. Then answer these questions in paragraph form on a separate sheet of paper. Indent the first sentence. Use capital letters and periods where necessary.

- What are Dan and Paul doing?
- What do they look at?
- What does Dan think of it?
- How can Dan afford it?
- How does Dan pay?
- Does he get a receipt from the cashier?
- What happens when he's leaving the store?

Dan and Paul are shopping for Mother's Day presents.

E. Discussion. What can happen if you don't get a receipt? Make a list of consequences.

➤ Do it yourself!

A. Write your own response. Then read each conversation out loud with a partner.

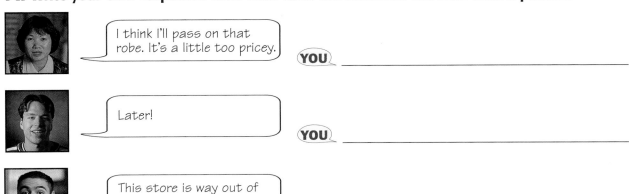

I think I'll pass on that robe. It's a little too pricey.

YOU _____

Later!

YOU _____

This store is way out of my price range!

YOU _____

B. Discussion. What do you think is going to happen next to Dan? Explain your idea.

Authentic practice

An arrest for shoplifting

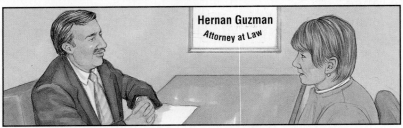

Hernan Guzman
Attorney at Law

A. Listening comprehension. Listen to the conversation. Then answer the questions.

1. Who are Mr. Guzman and Mrs. Ochoa? _____

2. Why are they having this discussion? _____

   _____

3. What will happen after this conversation? Make a list. _____

   _____

B. Read the statements. Listen to the conversation again. Then check *True, False,* or *?* (No information) for each statement.

	True	False	?
1. The conversation is in a courtroom.	❑	❑	❑
2. Dan Ochoa needs a lawyer.	❑	❑	❑
3. The cashier went to the cafeteria.	❑	❑	❑
4. Dan was arrested for shoplifting.	❑	❑	❑
5. Dan won't go to college in September.	❑	❑	❑

C. Vocabulary. Choose one of the words or phrases to complete each statement.

1. Taking something from a store without paying for it is _____.
   an arrest / shoplifting

2. A notice to appear in court is a _____.
   receipt / summons

3. A person who accompanies you to court to help you when you are arrested is a

   _____.
   police officer / lawyer

4. A person who didn't break the law is _____.
   guilty / innocent

92   Unit 7

D. Read Dan Ochoa's arrest record.

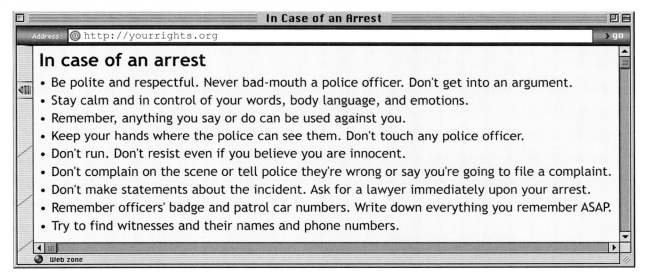

New Castle Police   CHARGE *Shoplifting*

DEFENDANT INFORMATION		

1. Name (Last, First, Middle) Ochoa, Daniel, Michael   **2. Alias / Nickname** Dan   **3. Phone number** 287-5065

4. Date of Birth 9 (Mo) 17 (Day) 1987 (Yr)   **5. Age** 17   **6. Sex** ☑M ☐F ☐U   **7. Race** ☑White ☐Black ☐Asian ☐Indian ☐Other ☐Unknown   **8. Ethnic** ☑Hispanic ☐Non-Hispanic ☐Unknown

9. Skin ☐Dark ☐Light ☑Medium ☐Other ☐Unknown   **10. Height** 5 (Feet) 10 (Inches)   **11. Weight** 158   **12. Hair** Brown   **13. Eyes** Brown   **14. Glasses** ☑No ☐Yes ☐Contacts

15. Build ☐Small ☑Med ☐Large   **16. Marital Status** ☐Married ☑Single ☐Common Law ☐Separated ☐Divorced ☐Widowed ☐Unk   **17. U.S. Citizen** ☑Yes ☐No ☐Unknown

18. Social Security No.   **19. Education**   **20. Religion**   **21. Occupation**   **22. Employed**   **23. Scars / Marks / Tattoos (Describe)**

E. Read the advice from a civil liberties Web site.

In Case of an Arrest

Address: @ http://yourrights.org   › go

In case of an arrest

- Be polite and respectful. Never bad-mouth a police officer. Don't get into an argument.
- Stay calm and in control of your words, body language, and emotions.
- Remember, anything you say or do can be used against you.
- Keep your hands where the police can see them. Don't touch any police officer.
- Don't run. Don't resist even if you believe you are innocent.
- Don't complain on the scene or tell police they're wrong or say you're going to file a complaint.
- Don't make statements about the incident. Ask for a lawyer immediately upon your arrest.
- Remember officers' badge and patrol car numbers. Write down everything you remember ASAP.
- Try to find witnesses and their names and phone numbers.

Web zone

F. Now read about Dan Ochoa's behavior. Compare his behavior with the advice on the Web site. Did Dan do the right things? What else should he do?

Dan didn't argue when he was arrested. He understood that it looked like he was guilty. He was polite and totally in control of his behavior. He went to the police station and quietly accepted the summons and agreed to appear in court. As soon as he got home, he wrote down everything that happened before and after the arrest. The next day his mother called an attorney to represent him at his trial.

➤ Do it yourself!

A. True story. Do you know a true story or a story from a book or a movie about a person who was arrested? Make notes.

- Who?
- What?
- When and where?
- Did the person follow the advice on the Web site?

B. Discussion. Use your notes to tell the story to your partner or your group.

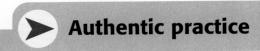

The elements of the U.S. justice system

A. Read the excerpt from a textbook of U.S. history.

The U.S. Constitution

In May 1787, the early leaders of this country met in Philadelphia to design the government of the United States. The document they created is called the Constitution. All the laws in this country are based on the Constitution. All new and old laws are examined to be sure they are "constitutional."

The Constitution tells us how the government is organized. It clearly lists and explains the powers of the government. It also explains the limits of the powers of the government.

We the People of the United States, in order to form a more perfect union, establish justice, insure domestic tranquility, provide for the common defense, promote the general welfare, and secure the blessings of liberty to ourselves and our posterity, do ordain and establish this Constitution for the United States of America.

The Bill of Rights

The Constitution gives the government power to make laws. Citizens have the responsibility of obeying those laws or facing punishment. But in order to protect citizens from unfair punishment, the Constitution also gives citizens certain rights. Those rights and protections are described in an important addition to the Constitution called the Bill of Rights. Below are a few of those rights that relate to the protections given citizens accused of crimes:

- The government or the police cannot search a house without permission. If the police think someone has committed a crime, they have to convince a judge of the court that the person is probably guilty. And if the judge believes the police, he or she will give the police a letter of permission to search the person's house. That permission is called a "warrant." Warrants protect citizens from unfair searches.
- A citizen accused of a crime is called a "defendant." Defendants have a right to a trial by a jury of impartial people, people who don't have an opinion yet about the facts. Defendants have the right to call witnesses who know the facts to help prove they are not guilty. Defendants also have the right to have a lawyer to help them at the trial.

One of the most important principles of our justice system is the "presumption of innocence." In every state, jurors are given instructions like these: The defendant enters this courtroom as an innocent person, and you must consider him or her to be an innocent person until the State (or the "government") convinces you beyond a reasonable doubt that he or she is guilty. The defendant does not have to prove his or her innocence. It is the State's responsibility to prove guilt.

42 *Our United States History*

Our United States History **43**

See page 148 for the complete Bill of Rights.

 FYI. For the complete Constitution and all its amendments, go to this Web site:

http://www.access.gpo.gov/congress/senate/constitution/toc.html

B. Vocabulary. Complete each statement with a word or phrase from the textbook excerpt on page 94.

1. The document that describes the organization and powers of the government is the _____.

2. Protections for citizens are contained in the _____.

3. A person who is innocent of a crime is not _____.

4. The _____ has the power to make laws.

5. The police cannot search a private house without a _____.

6. Only a _____ can give the police permission to search a house.

7. A _____ is a person accused of a crime.

8. A _____ is the process in which a person is judged guilty or not guilty.

9. Defendants have a right to a trial by a _____.

10. Jurors have to be _____. They haven't yet formed an opinion.

11. A person who knows the facts and can bring that information to the trial is a

    _____.

12. It is the state's responsibility to prove _____.

FYI. For a simple and understandable presentation of vocabulary that relates to the U.S. system of justice, go to this Web site:

http://www.usdoj.gov/usao/eousa/kidspage/glossary.html

C. Culture talk. How does the justice system in your home country differ from the justice system here? Compare and contrast cultures with your classmates. Give examples.

➤ Do it yourself!

Role-play. Role-play the trial of Dan Ochoa. First write questions that the attorneys might ask the defendant and the witnesses. Then role-play the trial.

Possible roles: Daniel Ochoa, the defendant
          Paul Yon, the defendant's friend, a witness
          Other witnesses: the cashier and the guard at Larson's Department Store
          Julia Ochoa, the defendant's mother
          Hernan Guzman, the defendant's attorney
          Marion Wilkens, the state's attorney
          Oliva Fernandez, the judge
          Jurors

Review

A. Pair work or group work.

Tell the story of Dan Ochoa's arrest and trial.

Ask and answer questions.

Create conversations.

Say as much as you can.

🎧 **B.** **Listening comprehension. Listen to Paul Yon's testimony. Then check *True, False,* or *?* (*No information*) for each statement.**

	True	False	?
1. Mr. Guzman asks how much the watch cost.	❏	❏	❏
2. Mr. Guzman asks how Dan paid for the watch.	❏	❏	❏
3. Paul doesn't remember how Dan paid.	❏	❏	❏
4. Paul didn't see a receipt.	❏	❏	❏
5. Paul is sure Dan paid for the watch.	❏	❏	❏
6. The cashier went to the restroom.	❏	❏	❏

🎧 **C.** **Listen to the first part of Paul Yon's testimony again. Then report Paul's answer in indirect speech.**

1. Mr. Guzman asked, "Now, Paul, could you please tell me where you were on Friday afternoon at about 4:45?" What did Paul say? _____

_____

2. Mr. Guzman asked, "Who, if anyone, were you with?" What did Paul say?

_____

D. **Read each sentence or question. Underline your response.**

1. "Are you in favor of censorship of books and movies?"

    YOU Under some circumstances.   **YOU** If it's not too pricey.

2. "I don't have any coins in the register."

    YOU That's OK. I have exact change.   **YOU** We'll have to agree to disagree.

3. "I could use a new watch."

    YOU Great. Let's go shopping.   **YOU** I think I'll pass.

4. "Here's another one for $59. What do you think?"

    YOU Awesome!   **YOU** I think it's morally wrong.

5. "This robe is $129. It's beautiful."

    YOU Just my luck.   **YOU** That's way out of my price range.

E. Punctuate each sentence or question. Use correct capitalization.

1. Mrs. Ochoa said my Danny never stole anything

2. Dan said I paid for the watch but I didn't get a receipt

3. Mr. Guzman asked Paul did you see Dan pay for the watch

4. Paul said Dan paid cash

F. Reread the excerpt on page 94. Then complete each statement with the correct word.

1. The _____ is a document that describes the organization of government and the rights of citizens.

2. In a trial, the person arrested for a crime is the _____.

3. The presumption of _____ ensures that defendants get a fair trial.

4. A letter of permission that allows the police to search a person's house is a

_____.

G. Composition. **On a separate sheet of paper, write about the picture on page 96. Say as much as you can.**

> **Now I can**
> ❑ discuss pros and cons of controversial issues.
> ❑ agree and disagree respectfully.
> ❑ report what other people say.
> ❑ understand the importance of the U.S. Constitution and the Bill of Rights.
> ❑ understand the elements of the U.S. justice system.

Health and safety

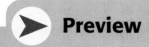

Preview

Warm up. Do you know what this chart is? What can you use it for?

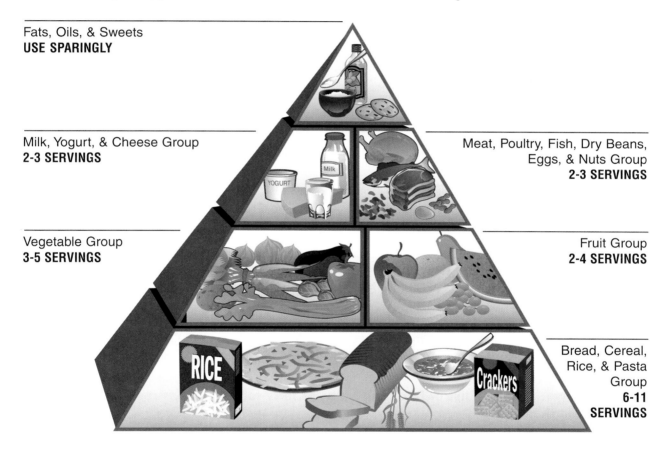

Fats, Oils, & Sweets
USE SPARINGLY

Milk, Yogurt, & Cheese Group
2-3 SERVINGS

Meat, Poultry, Fish, Dry Beans,
Eggs, & Nuts Group
2-3 SERVINGS

Vegetable Group
3-5 SERVINGS

Fruit Group
2-4 SERVINGS

Bread, Cereal,
Rice, & Pasta
Group
**6-11
SERVINGS**

Unit 8 objectives

- Express regret.
- Suggest a remedy.
- Avoid quackery.
- Separate weight-loss facts from myths.
- Make daily food choices based on the Food Guide Pyramid.

Practical conversations

Model 1   Express regret.

🎧 **A. Listen and read.**

    A: I shouldn't have eaten those pretzels.

    B: Why not? Didn't you like them?

    A: Are you kidding? Of course I did.
         But I have to limit my salt. I have
         high blood pressure.

    B: Oh, really? That's too bad.

🎧 **B. Pronunciation and intonation practice.**

🎧 **Vocabulary**

Ways to take care of health problems

I have to **watch my weight**. I'm overweight.	I have to **limit my salt**. I have high blood pressure.	I have to **stay away from fatty foods**. I have high cholesterol.

Another health problem and what you have to do: _____

C. Pair work. Make a list of fattening, salty, or fatty foods. Express regret about having eaten them.

fattening foods: *candy*
salty foods: *pretzels*
fatty foods: *meat*

    A: I shouldn't have eaten _____.

    B: Why not? Didn't you like _____?

    A: Are you kidding? Of course I did. But _____. I _____.

    B: _____.

A. Listen and read.

A: Don't you have migraines?
B: Yes, I do. Why?
A: They say Rackinusha cures them.
B: Really? Where did you hear that?
A: Right here. It couldn't hurt to give it a try.

B. Pronunciation and intonation practice.

C. Pair work. Choose an ailment from the ad or a real ailment. Suggest a remedy.

A: Don't you have _____?
B: Yes, I do. _____?
A: They say _____ cures _____.
B: _____?
A: _____. It couldn't hurt to give _____ a try.

Recently rediscovered in forgotten pyramid!

The miracle secret of the ancient Middle East–

RACKINUSHA

Cures migraines, arthritis, insomnia, nail fungus, psoriasis, and much much more!
➤ Completely natural
➤ Absolutely safe
➤ Available at drugstores everywhere

Stop suffering. Throw out all those useless medicines and get **RACKINUSHA** today!

OTC. No prescription necessary.

➤ Do it yourself!

A. Complete the chart with remedies you use.

Ailment	Remedy	Prescription required?	Effective?
colds	vitamin C	no	yes

B. Pair work. Compare remedies with a partner. Which is most effective?

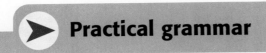

Practical grammar

Should have / shouldn't have

> Express regret for behavior with *should have* or *shouldn't have* and a past participle.
>
>   past participle   past participle
>
> I **shouldn't have** eaten that cake! I **should have** ordered fruit. It's much healthier.

A. Complete each sentence with a regret. Use *should have* or *shouldn't have* and a past participle.

1. You _shouldn't have bought_ all that candy. It's too hard to resist!
                    not buy

2. We _____ the soup. It looked great.
                    order

3. You _____ aspirin for that headache. It would be gone by now.
                    take

4. They _____ the fine print before spending all that money.
                    read

5. I _____ the doctor for a new prescription.
                    call

6. He _____ the whole cake! He has to watch his weight.
                    not eat

Negative *yes–no* questions

> Use a negative question to confirm information you think is correct or to ask for agreement.
>   Don't you have migraines?
>   Isn't that ad ridiculous?
>   Didn't you taste the chocolate cake?
> Sometimes the question also expresses surprise or disbelief.

B. Complete each negative *yes–no* question.

1. _Didn't you see_ the ad on TV last night?
         you / see

2. _____ better yet?
         it / be

3. _____ Rackinusha yet?
      the stores / have

4. _____ some herbal remedies were dangerous?
      the pharmacist / say

5. _____ usually _____ anything for her back pain?
         she / take

C. Complete each conversation with a negative question.

1. **A:** *Isn't the cake delicious* ?
   cake / be delicious

   B: Yes, it is. But it's too fattening for me.

2. **A:** _____ ?
   he / be a nurse

   B: Yes, he is. He works at General Hospital downtown.

3. **A:** _____ ?
   you / have insomnia

   B: Yes, I do. I never get enough sleep.

4. **A:** _____ ?
   that article on vitamins / be great

   B: Yes, it was. I learned a lot.

5. **A:** _____ ?
   you / try that new herbal remedy

   B: Yes, I did. It didn't work.

6. **A:** _____ ?
   you / ask your doctor about it

   B: Yes, I did, but he didn't know the answer.

7. **A:** _____ ?
   your sister / tell you about it

   B: Yes, she did. But I didn't believe it.

8. **A:** _____ ?
   it / work

   B: No, actually, it didn't.

➤ Do it yourself!

A. Complete the chart with two regrets about your recent behavior.

I should have	I shouldn't have
I should have bought milk yesterday. Now we're out.	*I shouldn't have drunk all that coffee after dinner!*

B. Pair work. Compare regrets with a partner.

Avoid quackery.

A. Discussion. Answer the questions. Then discuss with your classmates.

1. What's Sophie's problem? _____

2. What is she planning to do about her problem? _____

3. Does Helen think Sophie has a good plan? _____

4. What does Helen think Sophie should do instead? _____

B. Vocabulary. Find the underlined phrases in the picture story. Then check *True* or *False*.

	True	False
1. A <u>gullible</u> person believes everything he or she hears.	❑	❑
2. When you <u>send away</u> for something, you don't have it yet.	❑	❑
3. When you <u>pass up</u> food, you eat everything offered.	❑	❑
4. A <u>couch potato</u> doesn't exercise much.	❑	❑
5. When you <u>take someone's word</u>, you believe what he or she says.	❑	❑

C. Read each sentence or question. Underline your response.

1. "I just sent away for a miracle breakthrough."

   YOU You shouldn't have done that.   **YOU** Is it a couch potato?

2. "You can lose up to 30 pounds in the first week."

   YOU Come on!   **YOU** That's too bad.

3. "Don't you take my word for it?"

   YOU Are you kidding? Of course I do.   **YOU** I shouldn't have.

D. Reread the picture story. What are some of the claims the ad makes about Fat-B-Gone?

It says it works while you sleep.

E. Discussion. Discuss your answers to these questions with a partner or a group.

1. Have you ever heard of a product like Fat-B-Gone? Explain your answer.
2. What is a healthful diet? How much exercise is necessary or good?

➤ Do it yourself!

A. Write your own response. Then read each conversation out loud with a partner.

Look at this ad for a muscle-building machine! You don't have to exercise!   **YOU** _____

This cream is made from an ancient recipe, and it cures cancer!   **YOU** _____

Isn't it safe? It says it's completely natural.   **YOU** _____

B. Discussion. Find an ad for a miracle product. What claims does it make? Do you think it works?

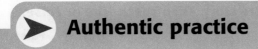

Nutrition, diet, and health

A. Take the self-test from *Body Wonderful* Magazine.

Body Wonderful Magazine

Self-Test
Dieting Facts and Myths

Test yourself on these common beliefs about diet and weight control.

FACT or MYTH? Check Fact or Myth next to each statement.

	FACT	MYTH
1. Skipping meals is a good way to lose weight.	❑	❑
2. Eating after 8 p.m. causes weight gain.	❑	❑
3. A good way to lose weight is to eat small meals throughout the day.	❑	❑
4. You need to use more calories than you eat to lose weight.	❑	❑
5. Certain foods, like grapefruit, celery, and cabbage, can burn fat and make you lose weight.	❑	❑
6. A "low-fat" label means the food has no calories.	❑	❑

B. **Listening comprehension. Listen to the report on nutrition and health.**

C. **Listen to the report again. Then check your answers on the self-test. (The answers are at the bottom of the page.)**

D. **Discussion. Compare answers with your classmates. Did the information surprise you? Which diet myths did you believe?**

FYI. More information on overweight can be found at this U.S. government Web site:

http://www.niddk.nih.gov/health/nutrit/pubs/statobes.htm

1. myth 2. myth 3. fact 4. fact 5. myth 6. myth

➤ Do it yourself!

A. **Study the food classes.**

🎧 **Vocabulary**

Classes of foods

fruits	vegetables	grains	fats and oils
sweets	dairy foods	meats	seafood

B. **Classification. Now complete this chart with foods you like. (Don't include prepared foods, like pizza, because it belongs to several categories.)**

Fruits	Vegetables	Grains	Fats/Oils

Sweets	Dairy foods	Meats	Seafood

C. **Discussion. In your opinion, which foods are healthful? Which foods are not healthful? Explain your reasons.**

Unit 8   107

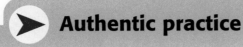
The Food Guide Pyramid

A. Look at the Food Guide Pyramid.

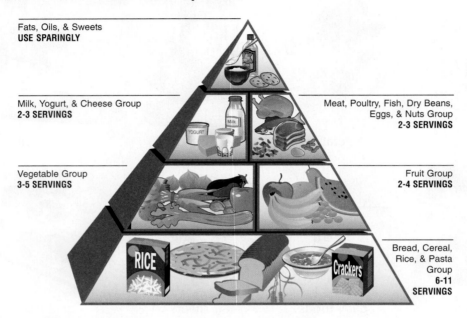

Fats, Oils, & Sweets
USE SPARINGLY

Milk, Yogurt, & Cheese Group
2-3 SERVINGS

Meat, Poultry, Fish, Dry Beans,
Eggs, & Nuts Group
2-3 SERVINGS

Vegetable Group
3-5 SERVINGS

Fruit Group
2-4 SERVINGS

Bread, Cereal,
Rice, & Pasta
Group
**6-11
SERVINGS**

B. Critical thinking. Discuss the answers to these questions.

1. What do you think is the purpose of the Food Guide Pyramid?

2. Can you explain why some foods are in the large bottom section of the Pyramid and other foods are in the small top section?

C. Write all the foods you ate yesterday.

Breakfast / Quantity	Lunch / Quantity	Dinner / Quantity	Snacks / Quantity
toast – 2 slices			

D. Discussion. Which part or parts of the Pyramid did most of your foods come from?

E. Read about the Food Guide Pyramid.

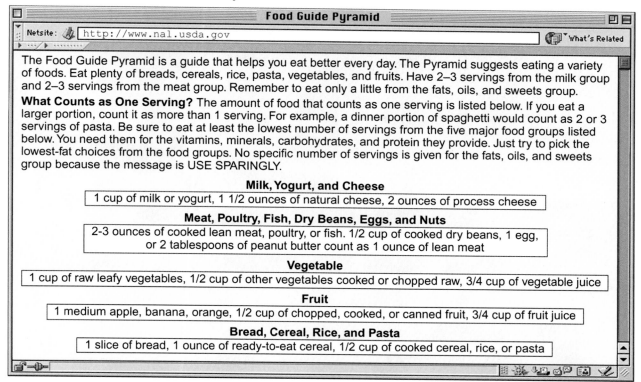

Food Guide Pyramid

Netsite: http://www.nal.usda.gov   What's Related

The Food Guide Pyramid is a guide that helps you eat better every day. The Pyramid suggests eating a variety of foods. Eat plenty of breads, cereals, rice, pasta, vegetables, and fruits. Have 2–3 servings from the milk group and 2–3 servings from the meat group. Remember to eat only a little from the fats, oils, and sweets group.

What Counts as One Serving? The amount of food that counts as one serving is listed below. If you eat a larger portion, count it as more than 1 serving. For example, a dinner portion of spaghetti would count as 2 or 3 servings of pasta. Be sure to eat at least the lowest number of servings from the five major food groups listed below. You need them for the vitamins, minerals, carbohydrates, and protein they provide. Just try to pick the lowest-fat choices from the food groups. No specific number of servings is given for the fats, oils, and sweets group because the message is USE SPARINGLY.

Milk, Yogurt, and Cheese
1 cup of milk or yogurt, 1 1/2 ounces of natural cheese, 2 ounces of process cheese

Meat, Poultry, Fish, Dry Beans, Eggs, and Nuts
2-3 ounces of cooked lean meat, poultry, or fish. 1/2 cup of cooked dry beans, 1 egg, or 2 tablespoons of peanut butter count as 1 ounce of lean meat

Vegetable
1 cup of raw leafy vegetables, 1/2 cup of other vegetables cooked or chopped raw, 3/4 cup of vegetable juice

Fruit
1 medium apple, banana, orange, 1/2 cup of chopped, cooked, or canned fruit, 3/4 cup of fruit juice

Bread, Cereal, Rice, and Pasta
1 slice of bread, 1 ounce of ready-to-eat cereal, 1/2 cup of cooked cereal, rice, or pasta

➤ Do it yourself!

A. Write a meal plan for yourself for tomorrow. Use the Pyramid.

Breakfast / Quantity	Lunch / Quantity	Dinner / Quantity	Snacks / Quantity

B. Discussion. Does your meal plan follow the guidelines of the Pyramid?

C. Culture talk. In the country you come from, what do people consider a healthful diet? Compare cultures with your classmates.

A. Pair work or group work.

• Who are the people?
• What are the problems?

Ask and answer questions.

Create conversations.

Tell a story.

Say as much as you can.

🎧 **B.** **Listening comprehension. Listen to the radio call-in show.**

🎧 **C.** **Listen again and match the dietary advice in column A with its purpose in column B, according to the radio program.**

	A		**B**
____	1.	Eat a variety of foods.	**a.** to avoid accidents and health problems
____	2.	Eat a lot of grains, fruits, and vegetables.	**b.** to avoid heart disease
____	3.	Exercise.	**c.** to maintain your weight
			d. to get necessary nutrients
____	4.	Don't eat a lot of fat and cholesterol.	**e.** to avoid high blood pressure
____	5.	Don't eat a lot of sugar.	**f.** to avoid eating a lot of fatty foods
____	6.	Don't eat a lot of salt.	**g.** to avoid tooth decay
____	7.	Don't drink a lot of alcohol.	

D. **Read each sentence or question. Underline your response.**

1. "Don't eat all that salt."

   YOU You're right. I have high blood pressure.   **YOU** You're right. I need some exercise.

2. "Why don't you buy some Fat-B-Gone?"

   YOU I'm not gullible!   **YOU** It's too fattening. I'm on a diet.

3. "If it's natural, it's safe!"

   YOU I think that's a myth.   **YOU** But it's so hard to pass up!

4. "You look terrific. How did you get in such great shape?"

   YOU I cut down on calories and started exercising.   **YOU** I sent away for it.

E. **Complete each sentence with a regret. Use *should have* or *shouldn't have* and a past participle.**

1. He _____ four servings of ice cream. You're supposed to eat ice
   (not eat)
   cream sparingly!

2. They _____ my word when I told them that Fat-B-Gone is a fraud.
   (take)

3. You _____ that silly ad about the muscle-building machine. No
   (not believe)
   pain, no gain.

4. I _____ my money on that cabbage-soup pill. Nothing burns fat.
   not waste

5. When I saw my doctor last week, I _____ her about those
   ask

   injections for my migraines.

F. Write two regrets that you have about your life. Use *should have* and *shouldn't have.*

   1. _____

   2. _____

G. Complete each conversation with a negative question.

   1. **A:** _____?
   celery / burn fat

      B: No. Take my word. It doesn't.

   2. **A:** _____?
   the Pyramid / be terrific

      B: Yes, it is. But it's a little complicated.

   3. **A:** _____?
   you / buy that muscle machine

      B: Are you kidding? Of course I didn't.

H. Composition. **On a separate sheet of paper, write about the picture on page 110. Say as much as you can.**

> **Now I can**
> ❏ express regret.
> ❏ suggest a remedy.
> ❏ avoid quackery.
> ❏ separate weight-loss facts from myths.
> ❏ make daily food choices based on the Food Guide Pyramid.

Preview

Warm up. Is this a good opportunity? Would you call 1-800-BIG-SIGN? Why or why not?

Unit 9 objectives

- Borrow money from a friend or co-worker.
- Agree to repay the loan.
- Remind a person to pay back a loan.
- Share wishes and dreams.
- Offer advice on financial aid.
- Understand work-at-home schemes.
- Understand credit unions.
- Understand the problems with payday loans.

Practical conversations

A. Listen and read.

A: I left my wallet at home. Do you think I could borrow $10?

B: Let me check what I have. Here you go.

A: Thanks so much. I'll pay you back tomorrow.

B: No problem.

B. Pronunciation and intonation practice.

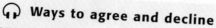

Ways to agree and decline

Agree: Here you go.

Decline: Actually, I'm short of cash myself. I'm sorry.

Vocabulary

Reasons to borrow money from a friend

I left my wallet at home.

I'm out of cash.

They won't accept my check.

I have to go to the cash machine.

They only take Master Charge or Quick Buy.

C. Pair work. Ask a friend for money.

A: _____. Do you think I could borrow $_____?

B: Let me check what I have. _____.

A: _____.

B: _____.

🎧 **A.** **Listen and read.**

> **A:** I'd love to go to college, but it's so expensive!
> **B:** Why don't you apply for a scholarship?
> **A:** Do you think that would be possible?
> **B:** You'll never know if you don't give it a try.

🎧 **B.** **Pronunciation and intonation practice.**

🎧 **Wishes and dreams**

go to college
get some more training
go to graduate or technical school

renovate my house
build a new garage
buy a new car

🎧 **Vocabulary**

Ways to fund dreams that are hard to afford

apply for a scholarship

apply for a college loan

get tuition assistance at work

borrow from the credit union at work

get a bank loan

finance the car

borrow money from your relatives

C. Pair work. **Share your wishes and dreams. Offer advice.**

> **A:** I'd love to _____, but it's so expensive!
> **B:** Why don't you _____?
> **A:** Do you think that would be possible?
> **B:** You'll never know if you don't give it a try.

➤ Do it yourself!

A. **Complete the chart with wishes and dreams.**

Wishes and dreams that cost money	Wishes and dreams that are free
I'd like central air conditioning.	I'd like to get married.

B. Discussion. **There's a saying that "the best things in life are free." Is that true?**

Common misspellings

Review the following spelling reminders. Don't make errors with these words.

they're, their, there

they're: They're writing a resume right now. (*they + are*)

their: It's **their** car. (possessive)

there: Look. It's right over **there**. (a place)

it's, its

it's: It's 5:15. Time to go home! (*it + is*)

its: The thing I like about this office is **its** location. (possessive)

then, than

then: First I called, and **then** I sent an e-mail. (a time)

than: This resume is newer **than** that one. (a comparison)

your, you're

your: This is **your** new office. (possessive)

you're: I hope **you're** happy here. (*you + are*)

two, too, to

two: I applied for **two** loans to help with tuition. (a number)

too: I wrote and I called **too**. (adds information)

to: It's too early **to** know if she got the job. (part of infinitive construction)

See page 144 for a more complete list of commonly misspelled words.

A. Choose the correct word to complete each sentence.

1. It's _____ loan, not my loan.
   they're / their / there

2. _____ OK. I can borrow from the credit union at work.
   It's / Its

3. A low-interest loan is better _____ a high-interest one.
   then / than

4. _____ late. The deadline for loan applications was yesterday.
   Your / You're

5. Those _____ offers are _____ good
   to / two / too   to / two / too

   _____ refuse!
   to / two / too

Connecting ideas with *but* and *so*

> You can connect two complete sentences with *and*. The second sentence presents additional information. Use a comma between the clauses.
>
> I asked for money. They lent it to me → I asked for money, **and they lent it to me**.
>
> Two other connecting words are *but* and *so*. Use *but* to introduce a clause with contradictory information. Use *so* to introduce a result clause.
>
> contradictory information
>
> I asked for money, **but they didn't lend it to me.**
>
> a result
>
> They didn't give me the loan, **so I borrowed the money from my family.**

B. Complete each sentence with *but* or *so*.

1. I wanted to finish my degree, _____ I applied for tuition assistance at work.

2. I work at Starlight Electric, _____ unfortunately they don't have a tuition assistance program.

3. Her lifelong dream was to have a pool, _____ she could never afford it.

4. She couldn't get a house with a pool, _____ she joined a health club.

5. He asked for $4,000 to build a garage, _____ it wasn't enough.

C. Complete each clause with contradictory information or a result.

1. I don't have enough money to get a new car, so _____.

2. I don't have enough money to get a new car, but _____.

3. The company they work for has terrible benefits, so _____.

4. The company they work for has terrible benefits, but _____.

➤ Do it yourself!

A. Revisit the wishes and dreams you wrote on page 115. Write a statement about each one with *but* or *so*.

I want to renovate my house, but it's very expensive.

I want to renovate my house, so I'm not taking a vacation this year.

_____

_____

B. Pair work. Compare statements with a partner.

Authentic practice

Work-at-home schemes

A. Read the picture story again. Answer the questions.

1. What kind of job are the people talking about? _____

2. What does the woman have to do before she begins making signs? _____

_____

B. Vocabulary. Choose the word or phrase closer in meaning to the underlined word or phrase.

1. Earn extra cash <u>in your free time</u>!

   ⓐ when you don't have to pay   ⓑ when you're not working

2. Well, this is <u>right up your alley</u>.

   ⓐ on your street   ⓑ just right for you

3. <u>Beats</u> an office job!

      ⓐ It's better than   ⓑ It costs less than

4. I'm calling to <u>find out</u> more.

      ⓐ learn   ⓑ look for

5. <u>Got it</u>.

      ⓐ I heard you.   ⓑ I know you.

6. Can I <u>put you down</u> for that?

      ⓐ insult you   ⓑ write your name on the list

7. On second thought, <u>never mind</u> the contract.

      ⓐ I want   ⓑ I don't want

8. <u>Suit yourself</u>.

      ⓐ You need to be well dressed.   ⓑ It's your choice.

C. Critical thinking. **Answer the questions. Then explain your opinions.**

1. What's good about the offer? _____

2. What's bad about the offer? _____

3. Should the woman take the offer? Why? Why not? _____

_____

➤ Do it yourself!

A. Write your own response. Then read the conversation out loud with a partner.

There's a low start-up fee of $5000. Can I put you down for that?

YOU _____

Do you have fax or e-mail?

YOU _____

You'd better act fast. After today, the fee is going up.

YOU _____

B. Discussion. **Have you ever heard of a work-at-home scheme? What were the terms? Did you get involved? Why or why not?**

Authentic practice

Loans

🎧 **A. Listening comprehension. Listen to the conversations about money.**

> January 15
> I promise to repay George Klagsbrun
> $450 by February 28.
>
> Melvin Clark

GET CASH UNTIL PAYDAY!
$100 or MORE . . . FAST.

Metro Credit Union ────────────────────── **MCU**

Consumer Loan Rates

New Car Loans
36 Months
5.5%

Used Car Loans
60 Months
5.75%*

Effective as of 7/1/04. Rates are based on term of loan. Additional discount may be available for automatic payment plan.

*Used Car Loan rates depend on the model year of the vehicle.

🎧 **B. Read the statements. Then listen to the conversations again and check *True*, *False*, or *?* (No information) for each statement.**

	True	False	?
Conversation 1			
1. They're talking about a bank loan.	☐	☐	☐
2. An IOU is a personal note in which someone promises to repay a loan.	☐	☐	☐
3. The man wants to buy a boat.	☐	☐	☐
Conversation 2			
1. They're talking about rates.	☐	☐	☐
2. A credit union is a car dealer.	☐	☐	☐
3. They want to buy a used car.	☐	☐	☐
Conversation 3			
1. They're talking about a paycheck.	☐	☐	☐
2. The woman wants to repaint her house.	☐	☐	☐
3. The woman needs cash.	☐	☐	☐

💻 **FYI. For a good glossary of credit and borrowing terms, log on to this Web site:**
http://www.cardreport.com/glossary.html

C. **Read the information about credit unions and payday loans taken from government Web sites.**

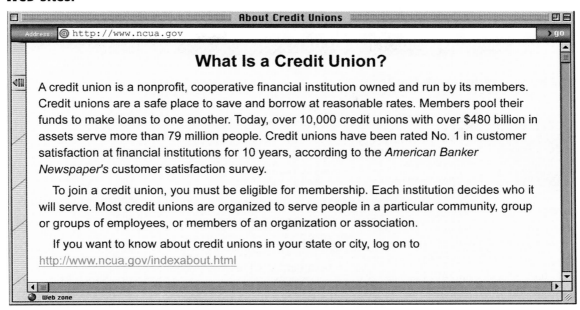

About Credit Unions

Address: @ http://www.ncua.gov

What Is a Credit Union?

A credit union is a nonprofit, cooperative financial institution owned and run by its members. Credit unions are a safe place to save and borrow at reasonable rates. Members pool their funds to make loans to one another. Today, over 10,000 credit unions with over $480 billion in assets serve more than 79 million people. Credit unions have been rated No. 1 in customer satisfaction at financial institutions for 10 years, according to the *American Banker Newspaper's* customer satisfaction survey.

To join a credit union, you must be eligible for membership. Each institution decides who it will serve. Most credit unions are organized to serve people in a particular community, group or groups of employees, or members of an organization or association.

If you want to know about credit unions in your state or city, log on to http://www.ncua.gov/indexabout.html

Web zone

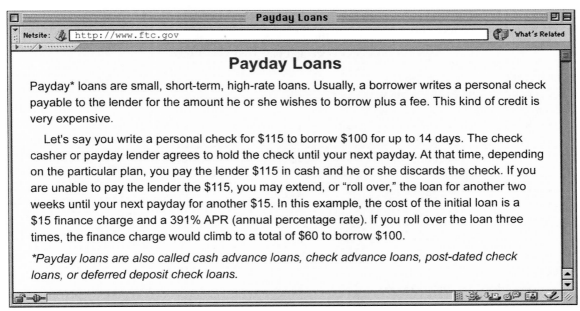

Payday Loans

Netsite: http://www.ftc.gov   What's Related

Payday Loans

Payday* loans are small, short-term, high-rate loans. Usually, a borrower writes a personal check payable to the lender for the amount he or she wishes to borrow plus a fee. This kind of credit is very expensive.

Let's say you write a personal check for $115 to borrow $100 for up to 14 days. The check casher or payday lender agrees to hold the check until your next payday. At that time, depending on the particular plan, you pay the lender $115 in cash and he or she discards the check. If you are unable to pay the lender the $115, you may extend, or "roll over," the loan for another two weeks until your next payday for another $15. In this example, the cost of the initial loan is a $15 finance charge and a 391% APR (annual percentage rate). If you roll over the loan three times, the finance charge would climb to a total of $60 to borrow $100.

Payday loans are also called cash advance loans, check advance loans, post-dated check loans, or deferred deposit check loans.

D. True story. **Have you ever borrowed money from a credit union or a friend? Have you ever taken out a payday loan, a personal loan, or a bank loan? Tell your story.**

➤ Do it yourself!

A. Discussion. **Discuss borrowing and lending.**

1. Is it sometimes necessary to borrow money?
2. When is it not a good idea to borrow money?

B. Culture talk. **Compare and contrast customs of borrowing and lending money in your home countries and here.**

"Neither a borrower nor a lender be."

🎧 **A.** Read and listen to the letters.

Ask Joan
Culture tips for newcomers

Dear Joan:
In my office there are a lot of people of different nationalities, and we have a tradition that's a lot of fun. Once a month, we go out to lunch to a different kind of restaurant—Chinese, Italian, Korean, Greek, Polish, Mexican, Cuban. You get the idea, Joan.

When the check comes, one co-worker (I'll call her Jenna) is always short a dollar or two, so she asks me to lend her the money. Jenna always forgets to pay me back. It's very hard to ask her to repay the money because it makes me feel stingy and unfriendly since it's only a dollar or two at a time. But I'm beginning to feel angry inside, and now I don't enjoy the lunches. Any advice?
Shelly, tired of shelling out

Dear Shelly:
It's awkward to ask friends or co-workers to pay back money you lent them, especially when it's only a small sum. But it's inconsiderate of Jenna to continue borrowing

without paying you back. I think you simply have to take the bull by the horns and say as politely as you can: "Jenna, it's really hard to ask you this, but do you think you could repay me the money I've been lending you when we go out? Even though it's only a dollar or two each time, it's starting to add up. I'd estimate that I've given you about $___ (fill in what you estimate the total is) by now, and I would feel a lot better if you could pay me back." Unless Jenna is a really terrible person, she'll apologize and pay. And you'll feel better that you spoke up!
Joan

Dear Joan:
I have not-so-great credit, and I made the mistake of borrowing money from a check-cashing place that gives payday loans. But the cost is exorbitant, and when you figure the yearly interest, it's more than 300%. Is that legal? What should I do?
Gullible Gus

Dear Gullible:
I haven't heard from you in a while. As you have learned the hard way, payday loans are <u>not</u> a

good way to borrow money. Read this information from the Federal Trade Commission regarding alternatives to payday loans:

> When you need credit, shop carefully. Compare offers. Look for the credit offer with the lowest APR (annual percentage rate). Consider
> - a small loan from your credit union or small loan company
> - an advance on pay from your employer
> - a loan from family or friends
>
> A cash advance on a credit card may also be a possibility, but it may have a higher interest rate than your other sources of funds. Find out the terms before you decide.
>
> Also, a local community-based organization may make small business loans to individuals.
>
> If you decide you must use a payday loan, borrow only as much as you can afford to pay with your next paycheck and still have enough to make it to the following payday.

Remember, Gus, to plan a budget so that you don't have to borrow money on a week-to-week basis.
Joan

B. Role play. Role-play a conversation in which you borrow money from a friend or co-worker and agree to repay. Then role-play a conversation in which the friend doesn't repay. Review the practical conversation on page 114 to enrich your role plays.

C. Discussion. Talk about different ways to get money. What are the pros and cons of each way?

Do it yourself!   A plan-ahead project

A. Read the ads.

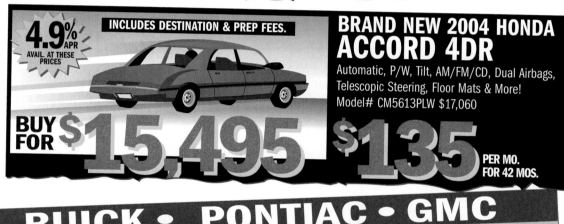

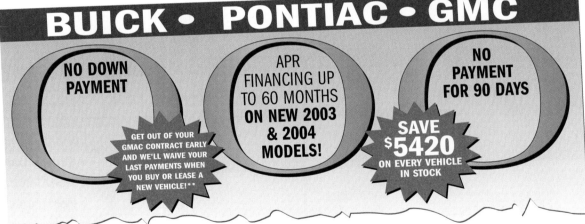

B. Find and bring in one or more items similar to the ones above:

- car ads from the newspaper to compare the terms of the loans
- ads for credit
- ads for work-at-home opportunities

C. Discussion. Compare what you found with your classmates.

Review

A. **Pair work or group work.**

- What is happening?
- What are the people doing?

Ask and answer questions.

Create conversations.

Tell a story.

Say as much as you can.

B. Listening comprehension. **Listen to the speakers. Then write your advice. Give reasons for your advice.**

1. My advice: _____

    _____

2. My advice: _____

    _____

C. Read each sentence. Underline your response.

1. "Here's a good opportunity for you. Telemarketing from home would be right up your alley."

   YOU But I have no e-mail.   **YOU** Really? How do I get started?

2. "My phone number is 325-0091."

   YOU Got it.   **YOU** I'm not that gullible.

3. "Never mind the offer. It doesn't sound good."

   YOU Suit yourself.   **YOU** There's a low start-up fee.

4. "I'd like to go to architecture school, but it's too expensive."

   YOU Have you applied for a   **YOU** I'll have to give this some
        scholarship?   thought.

D. Choose one of the words or phrases to complete each sentence.

1. When you ask another person for money and he or she gives it to you, you are

   _____ money.
       borrowing / lending

2. When you give someone money and he or she agrees to pay you back, you are

   _____ money.
       borrowing / lending

3. Money that you receive from a bank, a friend, or a relative and that you agree to

   repay is a _____.
                  loan / rate

4. A note in which one person agrees to repay another is _____.
                                        a payday loan / an IOU

5. _____ is money you owe to a lender in addition to the money
      A loan / Interest
   you borrowed.

E. **Complete each sentence with *but* or *so*.**

1. Joan advised Gus not to borrow money from a check-cashing business, _____ he went to the credit union instead.

2. The credit union offered much better terms, _____ Gus borrowed from them.

3. The check-cashing place and the credit union are both in the same neighborhood, _____ the credit union gives better terms on credit.

4. Mr. Santoro asked his sister-in-law for a loan, _____ she was short of cash and couldn't give him the money.

F. **Complete each sentence with a comma and a logical statement beginning with *but* or *so*.**

1. I needed money _____.

2. The bank advertised low rates _____.

3. The scholarship committee offered her a scholarship _____

   _____.

4. Gus saw an ad for a great work-at-home opportunity _____

   _____.

5. We didn't know the terms _____.

G. **Answer the questions.**

1. Why should you be careful of work-at-home offers? _____

   _____

2. Why should you be careful about payday loans? _____

   _____

3. What's the difference between getting a payday loan and borrowing money from a credit union or a bank? _____

   _____

H. **Composition. On a separate sheet of paper, write about the picture on page 124.**

> **Now I can**
> ❑ borrow money from a friend or co-worker.
> ❑ agree to repay the loan.
> ❑ remind a person to pay back a loan.
> ❑ share wishes and dreams.
> ❑ offer advice on financial aid.
> ❑ understand work-at-home schemes.
> ❑ understand credit unions.
> ❑ understand the problems with payday loans.

Your career

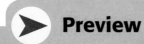

Preview

Warm up. Look at the resume. What's the purpose of a resume?

Carlos Sinkoff
uribres@mytimes.com
(201) 555-6743
45 McCabe Avenue, Hadley Beach, NJ 07865

OBJECTIVE
Position as an architectural draftsperson or commercial artist

SUMMARY OF QUALIFICATIONS
8 years of experience in the magazine publishing industry as an illustrator
4 years of experience in a civil engineering concern as a draftsperson

STRENGTHS
Visual creativity
Careful execution of projects on a timely basis

WORK EXPERIENCE
Elegant Interiors, Little Rumson, NJ
   Colorist and painter: 1998 to present

TAXI-FAST, Miramar, NJ
   Taxi driver: 1996-1998

Chilean Life Magazine, Osorno, Chile
   Illustrator and layout person: Full-time for two years, then part-time
   while full-time at Klimpft Associates: 1987-1995

Klimpft Associates, Temuco, Chile
   Chief draftsman in office of more than 200 architects and civil engineers:
   1991-1995

EDUCATION
   University of the West, Vina del Mar, Chile
   Bachelor of Arts, major in architectural drafting, minor in fine arts: 1987

REFERENCES
Available upon request

Unit 10 objectives

- Apply for a better job.
- Tell your employer about a job offer.
- Get a counteroffer.
- Give notice.
- Write a job history.
- Write a resume.

Practical conversations

🎧 **A.** **Listen and read.**

A: How long have you been in your current job?

B: Two years.

A: And why do you want to change jobs?

B: Well, I've completed my degree, and I'm ready for a bigger challenge.

A: That's great. Let's see what we have for you.

🎧 **B.** **Pronunciation and intonation practice.**

🎧 **Ideas**

Some reasons to apply for a better job

I've completed my degree, and I'm ready for a bigger challenge.

My husband / wife has been transferred here, and I need to find a new job.

My English has improved, and I'm ready for a professional job.

There's not much room to advance where I work now.

I'd like to make a career change, and that's impossible in my company.

Your own reason: _____

C. **Pair work.** **Explain why you'd like to change jobs. Use the resumes or your own resume.**

SCOTT FURILLO

2000 to present: Assistant front-desk manager, Kinkade Hotel, 3499 North Main, Medford, NJ 07080.

Marina Oxcraft

2002 to present: Bookkeeper, Accurate Accountancy, 12 Bank Street, White Plains, NY 10605.

Alan Petak

1996 to present: Service manager, German Motor Works, 3617 White Rock
                 Turnpike, Fairfield, CT 06432.

Anne Chang

1995 to present: Teacher's aide, Seattle Public Schools, 814 Fifth Avenue South, Seattle, WA 98109.

A: How long have you been in your current job?

B: _____.

A: And why do you want to change jobs?

B: Well, _____.

A: _____.

A. Listen and read.

A: John, do you have a moment to talk?

B: Sure, Oliva. What's on your mind?

A: Well, I've been offered another position. And I'm trying to decide what to do.

B: Really? Is there some way we can get you to stay?

A: Well, I don't know. They're offering a much higher salary.

B. Pronunciation and intonation practice.

Telling someone about a hard choice

I'm trying to decide what to do.
I've decided to take it.

I can't make up my mind.
The offer is just too good to refuse.

Vocabulary

Perks, benefits, and other features of good jobs

a higher salary   tuition assistance

more responsibility   better working conditions

more opportunity for growth   better benefits

C. Pair work. Talk about a job offer.

A: _____, do you have a moment to talk?

B: Sure, _____. What's on your mind?

A: Well, I've been offered another position. And _____.

B: Really? Is there some way we can get you to stay?

A: Well, I don't know. They're offering _____.

➤ Do it yourself!

Draft the beginning of your own resume. Begin with your name. Then add your last job and the date you began. Look at the resumes on page 128 as models.

_____
(Name)

_____ to present: _____

_____

The past unreal conditional

Explain consequences of unreal conditions in the past with the past unreal conditional.
Use *had* and a past participle in the *if* clause.
Use *would have* or *could have* + a past participle in the result clause.

> If Paul **had seen** that ad, he **would have applied** for the job. (But he didn't see the ad: unreal)
>
> I **wouldn't have studied** law **if** my mother **hadn't been** a lawyer. (But I did study law: unreal)

Don't use *would* or *could* in the *if* clause.

> ~~If Paul would have seen that ad~~…

A. **Distinguish between real and unreal conditions. Choose the statement closer in meaning to each underlined phrase.**

1. Al would have left <u>if they hadn't offered him an opportunity to advance</u>.

    ⓐ They offered him an opportunity.   ⓑ They didn't offer him an opportunity.

2. <u>If she had known about the job in quality control</u>, she would have taken it.

    ⓐ She knew about the job.   ⓑ She didn't know about the job.

3. <u>If they had told him about the promotion</u>, he would have accepted it.

    ⓐ They told him about the promotion.   ⓑ They didn't tell him about the promotion.

4. <u>If he had been there</u>, he could have told them about the opening.

    ⓐ He was there.   ⓑ He wasn't there.

5. The resume would have been better <u>if someone had helped her write it</u>.

    ⓐ Someone helped her write it.   ⓑ No one helped her write it.

B. **Choose the correct forms to complete each past unreal conditional sentence.**

1. What would you have done if they _____ you a promotion?

would have offered / had offered

2. If the opportunities to advance _____ better, would you have stayed?

would be / had been

3. If the company had offered a retirement plan, fewer employees _____.

would leave / would have left

4. If Ace Paints _____ a list of openings, they _____

would post / had posted

hadn't had / wouldn't have had

such a hard time hiring from within the company.

C. Complete each of the following past unreal conditional sentences.

1. If she ____*had applied*____ for that job, she ____*would have gotten*____ it.

   apply   get

2. If they _____ a better salary, more people _____

   offer   be

   available.

3. I _____ you if there _____ an opening in my

   interview   be

   department.

4. If they _____ me a better salary, they _____

   pay   convince

   me to stay.

5. If you _____ them your resume, they _____

   show   hire

   you on the spot.

6. If you _____ them your resume, you _____

   show   be hired

   on the spot.

➤ Do it yourself!

A. Speculate on what would have happened in your life if things had been different. Complete the sentences with true information about yourself.

1. If I had stayed in my home country, _____

   _____.

2. If my first language had been English, _____

   _____.

B. Collaborative activity. With your classmates, write your result clauses from Exercise A on the board.

Consider a counteroffer.

A. Check *True*, *False*, or *? (No information)* for each statement.

	True	False	?
1. Mike is a programmer.	☐	☐	☐
2. Mike's work is very good.	☐	☐	☐
3. Fred wants Mike to take the offer.	☐	☐	☐
4. Mike is going to take the Fischbach offer.	☐	☐	☐
5. Fred gets another job for Mike.	☐	☐	☐

B. Listen. Read each response out loud from the text.

C. Check the subjects Fred and Mike talk about.

☐ 1. a job offer from another company

☐ 2. a mistake Mike has made on the job

    ❑ **3.** problems at Fischbach

    ❑ **4.** a lack of opportunity for growth

    ❑ **5.** a possible counteroffer

D. **Read each sentence or question. Underline your response.**

1. "If I made a counteroffer, could I get you to reconsider?"

   YOU Forgive me for saying this.   **YOU** Possibly. There's no harm in trying.

2. "I'm going to have to give you notice."

   YOU I didn't see it.   **YOU** That's a shame.

3. "I'm sorry to spring this on you, but I've taken another job."

   YOU I appreciate the kind words.   **YOU** I'm not surprised.

4. "Thanks for the kind words."

   YOU You can take my word for that.   **YOU** For you? Anytime.

E. **Pair work. Take turns reading the items and responses in Exercise D.**

F. **Critical thinking. Answer the question. Then discuss your opinion with a partner or a group.**

What do you think Mike really wants? _____

➤ Do it yourself!

A. **Write your own response. Then read the conversation out loud with a partner.**

Would you be willing to consider a counteroffer?

YOU _____

It would be a shame to lose you.

YOU _____

If we'd known you wanted to move up, we would have offered you something sooner. Let me see what I can do.

YOU _____

B. **Culture talk. In the country where you come from, what do people do when they get an offer for another job? Role-play a conversation.**

Authentic practice

How to get a better job

A. **Listening comprehension. Listen to the conversations. Then answer the questions.**

1. Why is Sara unhappy at her job? _____

2. Why has Sara been underemployed in this country? _____

_____

B. **Read the statements. Then listen to the conversations again to complete each statement. Fill in the ovals.**

1. Sara is tired of _____.

   ⓐ Evan   ⓑ the assembly line

2. She has worked at her present job _____.

   ⓐ for two and a half years   ⓑ for two and a half months

3. Sara is afraid to tell Evan she wants a better job because _____.

   ⓐ he wouldn't have anyone to do her work   ⓑ her English isn't very good

4. When Sara speaks up, Evan _____.

   ⓐ says he will try to help   ⓑ is angry with her

5. In Venezuela, Sara was _____.

   ⓐ a manager   ⓑ an assembly-line worker

6. Sara's English is _____ now.

   ⓐ weaker   ⓑ better

C. **Role play. Role-play a conversation between two employees. One wants to move up but doesn't know how to make it happen.**

I'm ready to get a job with more responsibility. What should I do?

D. Culture talk. Compare the job you have now with the last job you had in your home country. If you are not working now, compare your life today with your life in your home country. Talk about how they are the same and how they are different.

➤ Do it yourself!

Look at the employment history section of a job application from a major company. Fill out the section for yourself. (*Note*: You may omit the section on salary for confidentiality.)

Employment History

List all employment since high school, including summer, cooperative education, and U.S. military service (you need to provide dates and relevant duties only). Start with your most recent position. Periods of unemployment should also be noted. Leave no gaps in time sequence. If you need more space, please use an additional sheet of paper.

Company Name				Type of Business		Company Address	Phone Number
Starting Date		Leaving Date		Starting Base Salary	Final Base Salary	Starting Position Title	Last Position Title
Mo	Yr	Mo.	Yr				
				$ wk yr	$ wk yr		

Name of immediate supervisor _____ Supervisor's position title _____

Reason for leaving _____

Please describe your duties and responsibilities _____

_____

_____

_____

May we contact that employer now? ☐ Yes ☐ No   If no, when? _____   Employer's Phone Number _____

Company Name				Type of Business		Company Address	Phone Number
Starting Date		Leaving Date		Starting Base Salary	Final Base Salary	Starting Position Title	Last Position Title
Mo	Yr	Mo.	Yr				
				$ wk yr	$ wk yr		

Name of immediate supervisor _____ Supervisor's position title _____

Reason for leaving _____

Please describe your duties and responsibilities _____

_____

_____

_____

May we contact that employer now? ☐ Yes ☐ No   If no, when? _____   Employer's Phone Number _____

Writing a resume

A. Read and listen to the letters.

Ask Joan

Culture tips for newcomers

Dear Joan:

In my country I was a commercial artist and draftsman. Eight years ago my employer went out of business, and I was having trouble finding work. But I was very lucky. I married a wonderful American woman and came to this country. My English was very bad when I got here, and I couldn't get work in my field. For the first two years I worked as a taxi driver. And since then, I've been working as a painter for a large company. The work is good, Joan, and I feel very lucky to be in such a wonderful country where there is so much opportunity, so I don't want you to feel sorry for me. But I speak good English now and I would like to go back to my profession. Do you have any advice for me?

Carlos Sinkoff

Dear Carlos:

Thank you for the kind words about this country! My advice to you, since you are seeking professional employment, is to write a resume. A resume is a brief presentation of your background, skills, and employment history. It is the traditional way to introduce yourself to a potential employer.

A reader sent me an article on resume tips from *Modern Professional* Magazine, and I've included it below. I hope it's helpful. I look forward to seeing your art in an advertisement or a magazine soon!

Joan

Modern Professional

■ Tips for a winning resume

Before setting off on that job hunt, polish up your resume to showcase your strengths and make yourself irresistible to an employer. The two most popular formats for resumes are chronological and functional.

Chronological: Lists work experience and education in chronological order, with the most recent dates first. It is common to subdivide the information into categories such as "work experience," "education," "professional affiliations," "languages," and "awards."

Functional: Organizes the information by skill and accomplishment areas. These do not have to be arranged chronologically. The functional resume is most effective for persons wishing to change careers or for persons who have not been in the job market for a number of years.

Resume red flags

Don't put the following on your resume:

- salary information
- reasons for leaving jobs
- personal statistics (weight, height, health, marital status, children)
- names of supervisors
- names and addresses of references

Above all: **BE ACCURATE, TRUTHFUL, AND DON'T MISSPELL ANYTHING!**

B. Critical thinking. Read the "Resume red flags." Why do you think it's not a good idea to put each one of those items on a resume? Discuss with your classmates.

C. Discussion. In your opinion, which kind of resume should Carlos Sinkoff write? Why?

➤ Do it yourself!

A. Look at Carlos Sinkoff's resume.

Carlos Sinkoff
uribres@mytimes.com
45 McCabe Avenue, Hadley Beach, NJ 07865

(201) 555-6743

OBJECTIVE
Position as an architectural draftsperson or commercial artist

SUMMARY OF QUALIFICATIONS
8 years of experience in the magazine publishing industry as an illustrator
4 years of experience in a civil engineering concern as a draftsperson

STRENGTHS
Visual creativity
Careful execution of projects on a timely basis

WORK EXPERIENCE
Elegant Interiors, Little Rumson, NJ
Colorist and painter: 1998 to present

TAXI-FAST, Miramar, NJ
Taxi driver: 1996-1998

Chilean Life Magazine, Osorno, Chile
Illustrator and layout person: Full-time for two years, then part-time
while full-time at Klimpft Associates: 1987-1995

Klimpft Associates, Temuco, Chile
Chief draftsman in office of more than 200 architects and civil engineers:
1991-1995

EDUCATION
University of the West, Vina del Mar, Chile
Bachelor of Arts, major in architectural drafting, minor in fine arts: 1987

REFERENCES
Available upon request

B. Write your own resume on a separate sheet of paper. You can use Carlos Sinkoff's resume as a model, or refer to the resume tips on page 136.

B. Listening comprehension. Listen to the conversations.

C. Read the statements. Then listen to the conversations again and check *True*, *False*, or *?* *(No information)* for each statement.

	True	False	?
1. Ms. Schacter saw an ad in the paper.	❑	❑	❑
2. She is currently working as a pharmacist.	❑	❑	❑
3. She is from Peru.	❑	❑	❑
4. She is married.	❑	❑	❑
5. She doesn't have a resume.	❑	❑	❑
6. She is going to study dentistry.	❑	❑	❑
7. She takes the job.	❑	❑	❑

D. Read each sentence or question. Underline your response.

1. "I can't believe you're taking another job!"

   YOU Yeah. Sorry to spring that on you.   **YOU** Forgive me for saying this.

2. "What kind of job are they offering?"

   YOU A resume.   **YOU** A high-level position.

3. "Why do you want to change jobs?"

   YOU I can't make up my mind.   **YOU** My husband was transferred.

4. "Would you be willing to consider a counteroffer?"

   YOU It would be a shame.   **YOU** No, the offer is just too good
   to refuse.

E. Distinguish between real and unreal conditions. Choose the statement closer in meaning to each underlined phrase.

1. He would have accepted the position if he had known about it.

   ⓐ He knew about it.   ⓑ He didn't know about it.

2. If she had written a chronological resume, they would have hired her.

   ⓐ She wrote a chronological resume.   ⓑ She didn't write a
   chronological resume.

3. <u>If you had included your supervisors</u>, your resume would have been too long.

    ⓐ You included your supervisors.   ⓑ You didn't include your supervisors.

4. You would never have gotten that job <u>if you hadn't written such a good resume</u>.

    ⓐ You wrote a good resume.   ⓑ You didn't write a good resume.

F. **Choose the correct forms to complete each past unreal conditional sentence.**

1. If she _____ in her resume, they _____ her the job.
            wouldn't send / hadn't sent   didn't give / wouldn't have given

2. If the company _____ earlier, they _____ a
                had known / would know   had made / would have made

   counteroffer.

G. **Composition. On a separate sheet of paper, write about the picture on page 138. Say as much as you can.**

> **Now I can**
> ❏ apply for a better job.
> ❏ tell my employer about a job offer.
> ❏ get a counteroffer.
> ❏ give notice.
> ❏ write a job history.
> ❏ write a resume.

This is an alphabetical list of all active vocabulary in *Ready to Go 4*. The numbers refer to the page on which the word first appears.

This is a unit-by-unit list of all the social language from the practical conversations in *Ready to Go 4*.

Unit 1

I'm collecting for _____.
Would you be willing to _____?
What did you say it was for?
I'd be happy to.
Thanks so much.
Hello?
Good evening.
Is this (a sales call)?
I'm sorry. (to refuse)
Thank you very much.

Unit 2

What's the problem?
I'm sorry. (to disagree)
OK. I'll see what I can do.
Hi, _____.
How's it going?
Not great.
(Our cable's) out.
I hope not.
I'll check and let you know.
Thanks.

Unit 3

I'm going to have to _____.
You're right.
I'm sorry. (to apologize)
Here you go.
I'll be back in (a few minutes).
Oh, no.
No, thank goodness.
Well, take it easy.

Unit 4

May I help you?
Hello. This is _____.
Would it be possible to _____?
Absolutely.

Right away.
Is there anything else?
Actually, . . .
Sure, no problem.
Is there some way we can make
   that up to you?
Of course.
Please accept my apology.

Unit 5

I don't believe it!
What?
I was supposed to _____.
Can I give you some advice?
You're right!
I missed it.
Would you like to _____?

Unit 6

Can you give me an estimate?
It'll be about ($500).
How long will it take?
Will you put that in writing?
Do you know (a good painter)?
As a matter of fact, I do.
Would you like me to _____?
That sounds like a good
   reference.

Unit 7

Are you in favor of _____?
What about you?
I'm against it.
I think it's wrong to _____.
We'll have to agree to disagree.
You want to know what I think?
I think it's ridiculous that _____.
You have a point.

Unit 8

I shouldn't have (eaten _____)!
Why not?
Didn't you like (them)?
Are you kidding?
Of course I did.
Oh, really?
That's too bad.
Don't you have (migraines)?
Yes, I do.
They say _____.
Really?
Right here.
It couldn't hurt to give it a try.

Unit 9

Do you think I could borrow
   ($10)?
Let me check what I have
I'll pay you back tomorrow.
I'd love to _____.
Why don't you _____?
Do you think that would be
   possible?
You'll never know if you don't
   give it a try.

Unit 10

How long have you been in your
   current job?
That's great.
Let's see what we have for you.
Do you have a moment to talk?
What's on your mind?
Is there some way we can get
   you to stay?

The following words are often misspelled, especially by people whose first language is not English. Pay particular attention to the words with an asterisk (*).

across	hundred	really	then
address	information*	receive	there
advice*	instead	recommend	therefore
afraid	its	referring	these
against	it's	responsibility	they
airplane	knowledge*	restaurant	this
all right	known	rhythm	thought
anything*	learn	right	thousand
behavior*	marriage	running	through
believe	maybe	Saturday	tomorrow
brought	medicine	scenery*	too
bury	men	science	traffic*
can't	minute	seat	traveling
choose	money*	sense	tried
chose	Mr.	separate	two
chosen	necessary	should	typical
clothes	neighbor	soccer	unforgettable
committee	occurred	somebody*	unfortunately
convenient	of course	something*	until
criticize	off	sometimes	used to
decide	opposite	special	usually
decision	paid	speech	very
describe	passed	spend	wait
destroy	people	spent	watch
didn't	physical	standard	wear
doesn't	plan	stopped	weather
don't	plane	story	were
effect	pleasant	strength	where
embarrass	possibility	studied	whether
etc.	possible	studying	which
everybody*	prefer	succeed	whole
everyone*	preferred	success	with
everything*	pretty	suddenly	without
exaggerate	privilege	summer	woman
excellent	profession	Sunday	women
exercise	professor	sugar	would
foreign	program	sure	writing
forty	pronunciation	surprise	written
fourth	proof	swimming	young
friend	psychology	taught	
grammar	quiet	than	
hear	quite	theater	
heard	read	their	* This word is always
heart	realize	themselves	singular. Never add –s.

144

The following verbs have irregular past-tense forms.

Base form	Past-tense form	Past participle	Base form	Past-tense form	Past participle
be	was / were	been	leave	left	left
begin	began	begun	let	let	let
break	broke	broken	lose	lost	lost
bring	brought	brought	make	made	made
buy	bought	bought	mean	meant	meant
can	could	been able to	meet	met	met
choose	chose	chosen	pay	paid	paid
come	came	come	put	put	put
do	did	done	read	read	read
drink	drank	drunk	ring	rang	rung
drive	drove	driven	run	ran	run
eat	ate	eaten	say	said	said
fall	fell	fallen	see	saw	seen
fight	fought	fought	sell	sold	sold
find	found	found	send	sent	sent
forget	forgot	forgotten	speak	spoke	spoken
get	got	gotten	take	took	taken
give	gave	given	tell	told	told
go	went	gone	think	thought	thought
have	had	had	understand	understood	understood
hear	heard	heard	wear	wore	worn
hurt	hurt	hurt	withdraw	withdrew	withdrawn
know	knew	known	write	wrote	written

Emotions	Mental states		The Senses		Appearances
adore	agree	know	feel	see	appear
appreciate	assume	mean	hear	sound	be
care	believe	mind	notice	smell	cost
detest	consider	realize	observe	taste	look
dislike	disagree	recognize	perceive		seem
doubt	estimate	remember			
fear	expect	see (understand)	**Preferences**		**Possession**
hate	feel (believe)	suppose	desire		belong
hope	find	suspect	need		contain
like	guess	think (believe)	prefer		have
love	hope	understand	want		own
regret	imagine	wonder	wish		
respect					

Verbs followed by gerunds

admit	discontinue	imagine	prohibit
appreciate	discuss	keep (continue)	quit
avoid	dislike	mention	recommend
can't help	enjoy	mind (object to)	report
can't stand	explain	miss	resist
consider	feel like	postpone	risk
delay	finish	practice	suggest
deny	give up (stop)	prevent	understand
detest			

Verbs followed by infinitives

afford	choose	learn	promise
agree	decide	manage	refuse
appear	deserve	need	seem
ask	expect	offer	struggle
arrange	fail	pay	volunteer
attempt	help	plan	want
can't afford	hope	prepare	wish
can't wait	hurry	pretend	would like

Verbs followed by gerunds or infinitives

begin	hate	love	start
can't stand	intend	prefer	stop
continue	like	remember	try
forget			

Verbs followed by objects and infinitives

advise	encourage	need*	require
allow	expect*	order	teach
ask*	force	pay*	tell
cause	help*	permit	want*
choose*	hire	promise*	warn
convince	invite	remind	would like*

* Words with an asterisk can also be followed by an infinitive without an object.

146

How to spell the gerund and the present participle

Add -ing to the simple (or "base") form of the verb.

     speak   →   speaking

If the simple form ends in -e, drop the -e and add -ing.

     have   →   having

In verbs of one syllable, if the last three letters are a consonant-vowel-consonant (C-V-C) series, double the last consonant and then add - ing.

     C V C
     ↓ ↓ ↓
     s i t   →   sitting

Exception: Don't double the last consonant in words that end in -w, -x, or -y.

     fix   →   fixing

In verbs of more than one syllable that end in a consonant-vowel-consonant series, double the last consonant *only* if the stress is on the last syllable.

     permít   →   permitting
     contról →   controlling
but not   órder   ordering

Internet sources for civics and consumer information

The following Internet sources are taken from the pages of *Ready to Go 4*. For fuller information, see the text and exercises on the indicated pages.

page 9: **www.ftc.gov** (telemarketing complaint form from the Federal Trade Commission)

page 11: **www.hud.gov** (information on volunteerism from the U.S. Department of Housing and Urban Development)

page 23: **www.apartments.about.com/ library/tools/bl_huntingchecklist.htm** (information on finding an apartment)

page 24: **www.hud.gov/offices/fheo/ FHLaws/index.cfm** (the Fair Housing Act from the U.S. Department of Housing and Urban Development)

page 53: **www.ftc.gov** (information on travel fraud from the Federal Trade Commission)

page 80: **www.bbb.org/bureaus** (consumer information on insurance from the Better Business Bureau)

page 80: **www.insurancefraud.org** (consumer information on insurance from the Coalition Against Insurance Fraud)

page 80: **www.iii.org** (consumer information on insurance from the Insurance Information Institute)

page 80: **www.ftc.gov** (consumer information on insurance from the Federal Trade Commission)

page 94: **www.access.gpo.gov/congress/ senate/constitution/toc.html** (the complete U.S. Constitution and amendments)

page 95: **www.usdoj.gov/usao/eousa/ kidspage/glossary.html** (glossary of terms relating to the U.S. justice system)

page 106: **www.niddk.nih.gov/health/ nutrit/pubs/statobes.htm** (information on overweight from the National Institute of Health)

page 108: **www.nal.usda.gov** (the Food Guide Pyramid from the U.S. Department of Agriculture)

page 120: **www.cardreport.com/glossary/ html** (glossary of credit and borrowing terms)

page 121: **www.ncua.gov** (information on credit unions from the National Credit Union Association)

page 121: **www.ftc.gov** (information on payday loans from the Federal Trade Commission)

The first 10 amendments to the Constitution were ratified on December 15, 1791 and form what is known as the Bill of Rights. The capitalization and punctuation in this version are from the original Bill of Rights, which is on permanent display in the Rotunda of the National Archives Building in Washington, DC. (See the National Archives and Records Administration Web site at **www.nara.gov**.)

Amendment I

Congress shall make no law respecting an establishment of religion, or prohibiting the free exercise thereof; or abridging the freedom of speech, or of the press; or the right of the people peaceably to assemble, and to petition the Government for a redress of grievances.

Amendment II

A well regulated Militia, being necessary to the security of a free State, the right of the people to keep and bear Arms, shall not be infringed.

Amendment III

No Soldier shall, in time of peace be quartered in any house, without the consent of the Owner, nor in time of war, but in a manner to be prescribed by law.

Amendment IV

The right of the people to be secure in their persons, houses, papers, and effects, against unreasonable searches and seizures, shall not be violated, and no Warrants shall issue, but upon probable cause, supported by Oath or affirmation, and particularly describing the place to be searched, and the persons or things to be seized.

Amendment V

No person shall be held to answer for a capital, or otherwise infamous crime, unless on a presentment or indictment of a Grand Jury, except in cases arising in the land or naval forces, or in the Militia, when in actual service in time of War or public danger; nor shall any person be subject for the same offence to be twice put in jeopardy of life or limb; nor shall be compelled in any criminal case to be a witness against himself, nor be deprived of life, liberty, or property, without due process of law; nor shall private property be taken for public use, without just compensation.

Amendment VI

In all criminal prosecutions, the accused shall enjoy the right to a speedy and public trial, by an impartial jury of the State and district wherein the crime shall have been committed, which district shall have been previously ascertained by law, and to be informed of the nature and cause of the accusation; to be confronted with the witnesses against him; to have compulsory process for obtaining witnesses in his favor, and to have the Assistance of Counsel for his defence.

Amendment VII

In suits at common law, where the value in controversy shall exceed twenty dollars, the right of trial by jury shall be preserved, and no fact tried by a jury, shall be otherwise reexamined in any Court of the United States, than according to the rules of the common law.

Amendment VIII

Excessive bail shall not be required, nor excessive fines imposed, nor cruel and unusual punishments inflicted.

Amendment IX

The enumeration in the Constitution, of certain rights, shall not be construed to deny or disparage others retained by the people.

Amendment X

The powers not delegated to the United States by the Constitution, nor prohibited by it to the States, are reserved to the States respectively, or to the people.

Grammar Booster

The simple present tense and the present continuous

The simple present tense

- Fact
  Many Americans **contribute** to charities.
  Some people **volunteer** for the fire department.

- Habitual action
  She **volunteers** at the shelter every week.
  Every night people **come** to the shelter for a place to sleep.

- With frequency adverbs: <u>often</u>, <u>never</u>, <u>always</u>, <u>sometimes</u>
  He often **collects** clothes for us.
  I never **give** money over the phone.

- With certain non-action verbs
  People **like** to help us.
  Charities **need** a lot of donations.

The present continuous

- An action in progress
  They **are distributing** the flyers now.
  She **is speaking** with the new volunteers at the moment.

The simple present tense	The present continuous
She **works** at the shelter every day.	She**'s working** with new volunteers now.
They often **make** phone calls for us.	They**'re making** phone calls right now.

Things to remember
Be careful! Don't use the present continuous with non-action verbs.
They need more money now.
NOT: ~~They are needing more money now.~~

A. Complete the sentences. Use the simple present tense or the present continuous.

1. In Mexico, people _____*speak*_____ Spanish.
   <small>speak</small>

2. Mrs. LeFevre _____ a blue uniform today.
   <small>wear</small>

3. Nurses _____ very hard.
   <small>work</small>

4. Ms. Rivera never _____ to work.
   <small>drive</small>

5. It _____ about 24 inches each year in Moscow.
   <small>rain</small>

6. We _____ now.
   <small>leave</small>

7. Mr. Hsie _____ on the phone right now.
   <small>talk</small>

8. The store usually _____ at 6:00.
   <small>close</small>

9. Most people in China _____ tea.
   <small>drink</small>

10. Millions of Americans _____ money or clothes to charities.
    <small>give</small>

B. Write questions or sentences in the simple present tense or the present continuous.

1. you / collect clothes / now?

   Are you collecting clothes now? _____

2. Mrs. Moreau / usually / bake cookies / for the bake sale.

   _____

3. where / Mr. Gaston / take / the donations / now?

   _____

4. the scholarship fund / always / give / money / to students.

   _____

5. the Kings / work at the shelter / now?

   _____

6. I / not want / to make phone calls / right now.

   _____

C. Complete the story. Use the simple present tense or the present continuous.

Every Saturday I _____ *volunteer* _____ at this homeless shelter.
                              1. volunteer

I _____ working here because I _____ a lot of
        2. like   **3. meet**

interesting people every day. Most of them _____ their own
                                                  4. not have

homes. Some people _____ at the shelter at night, but other
                          5. sleep

people only _____ here for the food and services. Every night,
                 6. come

about 50 people _____ here, and about 75 people
                      7. sleep

_____ here. Right now I _____ a writing class.
      8. eat   **9. teach**

My students _____ on their stories. They _____
                  10. work   **11. write**

about the hard choices we all _____ in our lives. My supervisor
                                    12. make

_____ the class today. He _____ my work is
      13. watch   **14. think**

important, and I do too.

1. The present perfect: <u>already</u>, <u>still</u>, <u>yet</u>, <u>ever</u>, and <u>never</u>

- <u>Already</u> is used in affirmative sentences. <u>Already</u> can come between <u>have</u> / <u>has</u> and the past participle.

    I have **already** fixed the toilet.

- <u>Already</u> can also come at the end of a clause or sentence.

    Yuji has arrived **already**.

- <u>Still</u> is used in negative sentences. <u>Still</u> comes between the subject and <u>haven't</u> / <u>hasn't</u>.

    Sonia **still** hasn't arrived.

- <u>Yet</u> is used in questions and negative sentences. <u>Yet</u> comes at the end of the question or sentence.

    Have they finished the job **yet**?
    No, they haven't finished it **yet**.

- <u>Ever</u> is used with <u>yes</u> / <u>no</u> questions. <u>Ever</u> comes between the subject and the past participle.

    Has she **ever** eaten there?

- <u>Never</u> is used for negative meaning. <u>Never</u> comes between <u>have</u> / <u>has</u> and the past participle.

    She has **never** eaten here.

A. **Complete the sentences with <u>already</u>, <u>yet</u>, <u>still</u>, <u>ever</u>, or <u>never</u>.**

1. I have ___*already*___ called the building manager.

2. Mr. Martinez has fixed this sink two times _____.

3. We've _____ had a fire in this apartment building. We've been lucky.

4. The plumber hasn't installed the new pipes _____.

5. And he _____ hasn't fixed the air conditioner.

6. Have the Corbos _____ lived in an apartment?

7. You _____ haven't given me your answer. When will I get it?

8. Has Yvonne _____ lived in Brazil?

- The present perfect is often used with <u>for</u> or <u>since</u>.

   Mr. Cha has been the landlord of this building **for** 10 years. [a period of time]
   He has been the landlord **since** 1998. [a stated time]

- Sometimes the present perfect and the present perfect continuous have the same meaning when used with <u>for</u> and <u>since</u>. This is especially true with the verbs <u>live</u>, <u>work</u>, <u>study</u>, and <u>teach</u>.

   We **have been living** here **for** seven years. = We**'ve lived** here **for** seven years.

- The present perfect continuous is often used for an activity that is still continuing.

   The landlord is **still** fixing the door.   The landlord **has been fixing** the door **for** three hours.

B. **Complete the story. Use <u>for</u> or <u>since</u>.**

   This is my house. I've lived here ___*for*___ 15 years with my husband and two
                                    1.

children. We've had our car _____ 1995. The Simone family has lived next door
                            2.

door _____ 12 years.
     3.

   I am an electrician. I've worked for the same company _____ July 2000. My
                                                          4.

husband has worked in his job _____ 20 years. We've saved $100 a month
                              5.

_____ 10 years.
   6.

   This year, my husband and I are going to take a vacation alone. It will be our

first vacation without our children _____ they were born!
                                    7.

C. Look at Marta's planner for this week. Complete the sentences, using the simple past tense, the present perfect, or the present perfect continuous.

	MONDAY	TUESDAY	WEDNESDAY	THURSDAY	FRIDAY
8:00 A.M.		Problem with the phone!—Call phone company	UNPACK!		UNPACK
9:00 A.M.	Pick up truck			Let phone company in to fix phone	
10:00 A.M.	Load truck with boxes		Buy microwave and toaster oven		
11:00 A.M.					
12:00 P.M.				Buy paint	Start painting kitchen
1:00 P.M.	MOVE IN!			UNPACK	
2:00 P.M.			Call phone company again		
3:00 P.M.		START TO UNPACK!			

1. Marta _____moved_____ to her new apartment on Monday.

move

   It's Tuesday morning. She _____ to unpack yet!

not start

2. It's Wednesday afternoon. She still has no phone service. She

   _____ the phone company two times since she moved.

call

3. It's Wednesday evening. Marta _____ a microwave today.

buy

4. It's Thursday night and Marta is still unpacking. She _____

unpack

   for three days.

5. It's 4:00 p.m. on Friday and Marta is still painting. She _____

paint

   the kitchen since 12:00.

6. It's almost the weekend. Marta _____ in her new

live

   apartment for five days.

1. Using gerunds

Gerund as subject
  Driving fast is dangerous.
  Not stopping at red lights is also dangerous.

Gerund as object of a verb
  I don't like **getting** parking tickets.
  I considered **not going** to the concert.

Gerund as object of a preposition
  Some drivers aren't good at **parking** in the city.
  She's upset about **not being invited** to the meeting.

Gerund as complement
  The worst thing about traffic is **honking**.
  The thing I hate about being late is **not getting** a good parking spot.

Things to remember
1. The gerund has the same form as the present participle. See page 147 for how to spell the gerund and the present participle.
2. Form the negative of a gerund by adding <u>not</u> before the gerund.

A. Complete the sentences. Use a gerund form of a word or phrase from the box.

be polite	drive	listen	not signal	not stop
pass	~~speed~~	tailgate	talk	walk

1. Mr. Chen got a ticket for _____*speeding*_____.

2. _____ to police officers is important. If you're rude to them, you'll get in trouble.

3. _____ on the right is against the law. It is also very dangerous.

4. _____ is dangerous because cars can stop suddenly in traffic.

5. Some states have laws against _____ on a handheld cell phone while driving.

6. _____ without a license is illegal.

7. _____ at a stop sign can cause a serious accident.

8. They enjoy _____ to music when they drive.

9. Instead of _____, let's take the bus. We'll get there faster.

10. After he turned the corner, the police stopped him for _____.

B. Look at the signs. Complete the sentences with a gerund.

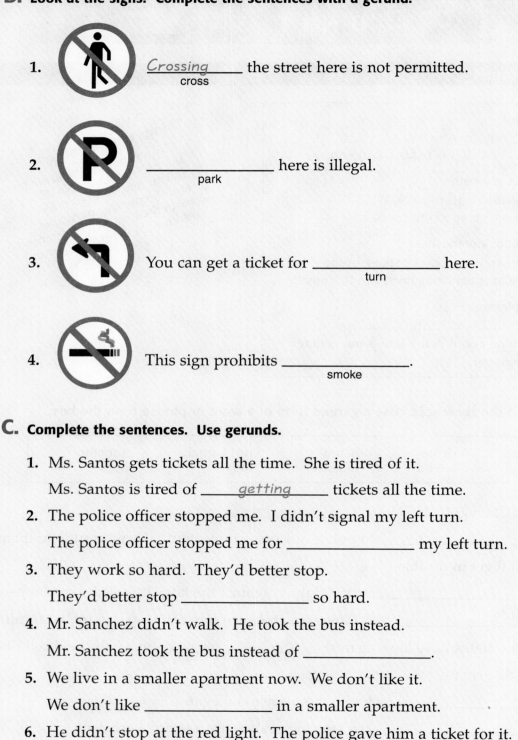

1. *Crossing* the street here is not permitted.
   cross

2. _____ here is illegal.
   park

3. You can get a ticket for _____ here.
   turn

4. This sign prohibits _____.
   smoke

C. Complete the sentences. Use gerunds.

1. Ms. Santos gets tickets all the time. She is tired of it.

   Ms. Santos is tired of _____*getting*_____ tickets all the time.

2. The police officer stopped me. I didn't signal my left turn.

   The police officer stopped me for _____ my left turn.

3. They work so hard. They'd better stop.

   They'd better stop _____ so hard.

4. Mr. Sanchez didn't walk. He took the bus instead.

   Mr. Sanchez took the bus instead of _____.

5. We live in a smaller apartment now. We don't like it.

   We don't like _____ in a smaller apartment.

6. He didn't stop at the red light. The police gave him a ticket for it.

   The police gave him a ticket for _____ at the red light.

2. Infinitives of purpose

Infinitives of purpose

Why did you go to the office yesterday?
To talk to my teacher.

Why did he stop at the gas station?
To ask for directions.

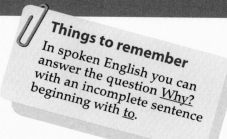

Things to remember
In spoken English you can answer the question <u>Why?</u> with an incomplete sentence beginning with <u>to</u>.

D. **Combine the following sentences. Use infinitives of purpose.**

1. Mr. Yi went to the post office. He needed to get some stamps.

   <u>Mr. Yi went to the post office to get some stamps.</u>

2. We had a party. We were welcoming our new neighbors.

   _____

3. I visited my friend at the hospital. I saw her new baby.

   _____

4. Masa came over. He picked us up.

   _____

E. **Look at Gilda's plans. Answer the questions with infinitives of purpose.**

Plan #1: Go to community college:
   —Fill out an application for South Community
      College (SCC)
   —Call SCC for appointment with counselor

Plan #2: Buy a car:
   —Apply for a loan at Crane Bank

Plan #3: Get in shape—lose 10 pounds:
   —Walk every day
   —Stop eating dessert

1. Why is Gilda going to fill out an application? <u>to go to SCC community college</u>

2. Why is she going to call SCC? _____

3. Why is Gilda applying for a loan? _____

4. Why is she going to walk every day? _____

5. Why is she going to stop eating dessert? _____

3. Verbs followed by infinitives (review)

Some verbs, such as <u>decide</u>, <u>forget</u>, <u>need</u>, <u>plan</u>, <u>remember</u>, and <u>want</u>, use the infinitive:

He got a ticket because he forgot **to signal**.
I planned **to get** there early, but the traffic was very bad.

F. **Complete the sentences with a gerund or an infinitive.**

Carla plans _____*to get*_____ her driver's license soon. She got a book from
_{1. get}

the Department of Motor Vehicles _____ for her test. She is tired of
_{2. study}

_____ the book and wants _____ her driving more.
_{3. read}   _{4. practice}

Carla enjoys _____ a lot. She remembers _____ on
_{5. drive}   _{6. pass}

the left, but she sometimes forgets _____ before she turns. Her
_{7. signal}

driving instructor has told her to stop _____, but she keeps
_{8. tailgate}

_____ it.
_{9. do}

Next week, Carla will go to the Department of Motor Vehicles _____
_{10. take}

her driving test. She can't wait!

UNIT 4

Some and any

> ### Some and any
> They need **some** soap.
> They don't need **any** shampoo.
>
> Do you want **any** ice?   No, thank you, I don't want **any**.
> Are there **any** towels?   Yes, there are **some** in the closet.

A. Complete the sentences. Use <u>some</u> or <u>any</u>.

1. There is __*some*__ juice in the refrigerator, but there isn't __*any*__ milk.

2. I didn't bring _____ soap, but I brought _____ shampoo.

3. Henry needs _____ towels, and he didn't bring _____ washcloths.

4. They didn't ask for _____ food, but they asked for _____ beverages.

5. Ms. Patel wanted _____ sugar, but she didn't want _____ milk.

6. We ordered _____ breakfast, but we didn't order _____ coffee.

7. I don't have _____ newspapers at home, but I have _____ magazines.

8. There is _____ paper in the closet, but there aren't _____ pencils.

B. Complete the note with <u>some</u> or <u>any</u>.

Nida,

   I need __*some*__ help to get ready for the training tomorrow. We have
         1.

_____ photocopies of the handout, but we need _____ more, maybe 50 of
   2.   **3.**

each page. The room doesn't have _____ chairs, and I think we need _____
                                      4.   **5.**

tables too. Please ask for _____ glasses for water. There aren't _____
                              6.   **7.**

pens or pencils in the room yet, and we need _____ paper for each person.
                                                 8.

Also, please see if you can get _____ name tags.
                                    9.

Thanks,

Greta

C. Complete the conversations. Use <u>some</u> or <u>any</u>.

1. **A:** Does he need any paper towels?

   B: No, <u> he doesn't need any </u>.

   He needs _____ <u>some</u> _____ trashbags.

2. **A:** _____ ice?

   B: Yes, please. And we need some more glasses.

3. **A:** _____ beverages?

   B: No, she didn't. She ordered soup.

4. **A:** Did they get any fruit?

   B: No, _____ vegetables.

5. **A:** Is there any coffee left?

   B: No, but _____ tea.

6. **A:** Do you need any assistance?

   B: No, thanks, I _____.

7. **A:** _____ milk?

   B: No, there isn't. We need to buy some.

8. **A:** Are there any cookies?

   B: Yes, _____ on the table.

9. **A:** _____ shampoo?

   B: No, they didn't. They just bought

   _____ aspirin.

10. **A:** _____ hangers, please?

    B: Sure. Is there anything else I can get for you?

1. Conditional sentences

- Real conditionals are used to state conditions that exist.

  If she has the money, she'll buy the car. [real condition, real result]

- Unreal conditionals are used to state conditions that don't exist.

  If he were rich, he would buy a house. [But he isn't rich—unreal condition, unreal result]

- In real conditionals, use the simple present tense in the <u>if</u> clause, and a future form in the result clause.

  If she **has** the money, she**'ll buy** the car.
  If you **forget** the forms, you **won't be allowed to** register.

- In unreal conditionals, use the simple past tense in the <u>if</u> clause. Use <u>would</u> or <u>could</u> and the base form of the verb in the result clause.

  If they **had** more time, they **could stop** for lunch.

- In unreal conditionals, use <u>were</u> for all forms of <u>be</u> in the <u>if</u> clause.

  If I **were** younger, I would travel around the world.

Things to remember

Be careful: Never use <u>would</u> in the <u>if</u> clause.

If I knew his name, I would tell you.

NOT: ~~If I would know his name~~, I would tell you.

A. **Read the conditional sentences. Decide whether the sentences are real or unreal conditionals. Write <u>R</u> next to the real conditionals and <u>U</u> next to the unreal conditionals. Then complete the sentences with the correct verb form.**

<u>R</u> 1. If it rains tomorrow, I <u>'ll wear</u> a raincoat.
                                      wear

____ 2. If Mr. Benitez had a car, he _____.
                                           drive

____ 3. If the office is closed, I _____ them tomorrow.
                                        call

____ 4. If I were taller, I _____ the shelf.
                                 reach

____ 5. If they wanted to, they _____ here on time.
                                      get

____ 6. If the phone rings, I _____ it.
                                   answer

____ 7. If Linda paid more attention in class, she _____ better on the tests.
                                                          do

____ 8. If Paul asks her, she _____ him.
                                   marry

____ 9. If we leave now, we _____ there on time.
                                 get

____ 10. If I get any more tickets, I _____ my driver's license.
                                           lose

2. Conditional questions

REAL CONDITIONS

Question word	Will	Subject	Base form of the verb	If clause
	Will	she	go home	**if** she **finishes** all her work?
Where	**will**	you	live	**if** you **don't get** the apartment?

UNREAL CONDITIONS

Question word	Would	Subject	Base form of the verb	If clause
	Would	she	call	**if** she **were** in town?
What	**would**	you	do	**if** you **lost** your job?

B. **Change the sentences into questions.**

1. If you needed to meet the deadline, you would work long hours.

   Would you work long hours if you needed to meet the deadline?

2. Marcel would be happier if he lived closer to his family.

   _____

3. They'll go on a trip if they get the time off.

   _____

4. If they had the money, they would go to a better school.

   _____

5. You have to pay a fine if you return a library book late.

   _____

6. If the store gives her a discount, she'll buy the TV today.

   _____

3. Order of clauses in conditional sentences

If clause	Result
If you invite him,	he will come.
If we drove,	it would be faster.

Result	If clause
He will come	**if you invite him.**
It would be faster	**if we drove.**

Things to remember

When the <u>if</u> clause is first in the sentence, use a comma. Do not use a comma when the <u>if</u> clause comes last.

C. Combine the sentences to make unreal or real conditionals. Write each sentence two ways.

1. We don't have heat. We aren't warm. (unreal)

   If we had heat, we would be warm.

   We would be warm if we had heat.

2. Ms. Alvarez is late. She has to reschedule the appointment. (real)

   If Ms. Alvarez is late, she will have to reschedule the appointment.

   Ms. Alvarez _____

3. I pay my bills on time. I don't have to pay interest. (unreal)

   _____

   _____

4. Mr. Marin has two jobs. He has enough money to move. (unreal)

   _____

   _____

5. The store is open. I'll return the toaster. (unreal)

   _____

   _____

6. The weather is good. I'll go to the beach. (real)

   _____

   _____

   _____

   _____

1. The sentence

> • A sentence must have a subject and a verb and must express a complete idea.
>   It must also begin with a capital letter and end with a period.
>   **Subject   Verb**
>   **The painter gave** me a reasonable estimate. [expresses a complete idea]
>
> • Study these examples of incomplete sentences:
>   An estimate for electrical work. [a subject, but not a verb = not a complete idea]
>   Is doing a very efficient job. [a verb, but not a subject = not a complete idea]
>   He is doing. [a verb and a subject, but not a complete idea]

A. Write the subject and verb for each sentence on the lines.

	Subject	**Verb**
1. We have class today.	*We*	*have*
2. Fifteen students were late.	_____	_____
3. Some electrical work is dangerous.	_____	_____
4. Mr. Rios put the estimate in writing.	_____	_____
5. His paint job took a long time.	_____	_____
6. The mover drove too fast.	_____	_____

B. Write <u>S</u> next to the groups of words that are sentences. If it is not a sentence, write the reason: <u>No subject</u>, <u>No verb</u>, or <u>Subject and verb, but not a complete idea</u>.

____ 1. The tall man took.   *Subject and verb, but not a complete idea*

____ 2. I was getting.   _____

____ 3. Mr. Carson put.   _____

____ 4. We saw a movie.   _____

____ 5. If she knew.   _____

____ 6. You can't find them.   _____

____ 7. Is under the desk.   _____

____ 8. The store yesterday.   _____

____ 9. She was here.   _____

____ 10. The biggest building
          in town.   _____

2. Other punctuation rules

- After abbreviated titles (<u>Mr.</u>, <u>Mrs.</u>, <u>Ms.</u>, <u>Dr.</u>, etc.), use a period. (<u>Miss</u> is not an abbreviation, so it does not use a period.) Capitalize the first letter of the word of the title.

- Capitalize the names of streets (<u>Main Street</u>, <u>Martin Luther King, Jr. Boulevard</u>). If you abbreviate the words <u>Street</u>, <u>Road</u>, <u>Avenue</u>, <u>Boulevard</u>, etc., use a period after the abbreviation (<u>Main St.</u>, <u>Martin Luther King, Jr. Blvd.</u>)

- All states have a two-letter postal abbreviation, such as <u>NY</u>, <u>TX</u>, <u>CA</u>, <u>MA</u>, and <u>CO</u>. Capitalize both letters. Do not use periods.

C. **Address an envelope to each of the people in the list below. Use correct capitalization and punctuation.**

1. mr hugo grenier	770 high st	alexandria va 22301
2. ms diana morales	1832 south tulip st	bradenton fl 34282
3. dr lydia park	643 west ave	cambridge ma 02138
4. mr and mrs lee	22 main st	san mateo ca 94402

1.

M. Smith
10 Main St.
Centerville, NY 10101

Mr. Hugo Grenier
770 High St.
Alexandria, VA 22301

3.

M. Smith
10 Main St.
Centerville, NY 10101

2.

M. Smith
10 Main St.
Centerville, NY 10101

4.

M. Smith
10 Main St.
Centerville, NY 10101

D. **Put the words in order. Write sentences or questions. Use correct capitalization and punctuation.**

1. amarillo texas / my sister / in / is

   My sister is in Amarillo, Texas.

2. lives / his doctor/ miami / in / florida

   _____

3. did / new york / do / what / they / in

   _____

4. south africa / in / mr burcos / does / live

   _____

5. pat's cleaning supplies / is / the address / for / 23 pine street

   _____

UNIT 7

1. Reporting a person's words: direct speech

> **Direct speech**
> Sara said, "I agree with the new smoking laws."
> Tom asked, "Why are there laws about smoking?"
> Jake said, "That's a beautiful building!"

A. **Insert a comma, quotation marks, and a period or a question mark in each of the following.**

1. Julia asked, "Are you ready to go?"
2. I answered   No, I have to finish writing this report
3. She said   I will wait for you
4. I asked   Where do you want to eat
5. She answered   I'd like to try The Fish Market
6. I said   That sounds good
7. Julia said   Rob said the desserts are delicious
8. I asked   When did you talk to Rob

B. Rewrite the quoted speech with correct punctuation and capitalization. Use commas, periods, question marks, quotation marks, and the verbs <u>asked</u> or <u>said</u>.

1. Will: what do you think about movie ratings

   Will asked, "What do you think about movie ratings?"

2. Sergei: I think it's wrong to have them

   _____

3. Donna: I think some movies are too violent for children

   _____

4. Sergei: I agree, and also some language and topics are not appropriate for children

   _____

5. Will: do you think that the movie industry should rate movies

   _____

6. Donna: the rating system helps parents decide which movies their children should see

   _____

7. Sergei: parents, not the movie industry, should choose movies for their children

   _____

8. Will: if you're over 16, you should be able to watch whatever movie you want

   _____

2. Reporting a person's words: Indirect speech

Direct speech

Mr. Morales says, **"**The landlord has to fix my front door.**"**

Ms. Young says, **"**I need a new job.**"**

Indirect speech

Mr. Morales says (that) the landlord has to fix his front door.

Ms. Young says (that) she needs a new job.

Changes from direct to indirect speech

Mary says, **"**I **don't** agree.**"**

Mary says (that) she **doesn't** agree.

Carlos says, **"**I **want** to talk to my boss about a raise today.**"**

Carlos says (that) he **wants** to talk to his boss about a raise today.

Things to remember

1. In indirect speech, changes in pronouns and possessive adjectives are made to keep the speaker's original meaning. For example, the subject pronoun I changes to <u>he</u> or <u>she</u>, <u>you</u> changes to <u>I</u> or <u>we</u>, and the possessive adjective <u>my</u> changes to <u>his</u> or <u>her</u>, and <u>our</u> changes to <u>their</u>.

2. The verb form in indirect speech also changes according to the changes in the subject pronoun. Tom says, "I'm ready to leave." Tom says <u>he's</u> ready to leave.

C. Rewrite the following sentences in indirect speech.

1. Ken says, "I need to find my coat."

   Ken says that he needs to find his coat.

2. Ms. Sierra says, "I don't have my receipt."

   _____

3. The officer says, "You have to wait here."

   _____

4. The salesperson says, "You can't smoke in the building."

   _____

5. Mr. Kim says, "I can't find my wallet."

   _____

D. Report what each person says. Write it on the lines.

People should be able to smoke anywhere.

Ali

The government shouldn't tell me where I can smoke.

Grace

If I want to smoke, it's my decision.

Robert

I don't think smoking is a right because it affects other people, too.

Maurice

It's great that I can eat in a restaurant without smelling smoke.

Claudia

If you want to smoke, you should do it far from other people.

Anna

1. Ali _____ *says that people should be able to smoke anywhere* _____.

2. Robert _____.

3. Claudia _____.

4. Grace _____.

5. Maurice _____.

6. Anna _____.

1. Should have / shouldn't have

Subject	should / shouldn't	have	Past participle	
I You He They	should shouldn't	have	called eaten	early. so much.

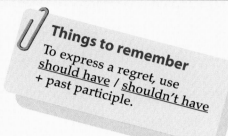

Things to remember
To express a regret, use <u>should have</u> / <u>shouldn't have</u> + past participle.

A. **Complete each sentence with a regret. Use <u>should have</u> or <u>shouldn't have</u> and a past participle. Use the verbs in the box.**

buy	~~call~~	drink	eat	go	read	spend	study

1. Marie ___should have called___ her father on his birthday.

2. We _____ so much money.

3. I _____ to the dentist last week. If I had,
   I would be better by now.

4. The Moons _____ at Joe's Diner instead of
   The Malibu Café. Everything at Joe's is cheap and good.

5. He _____ coffee. Now he feels very nervous.

6. You _____ the directions. You needed to
   take that pill with food.

7. She _____ that new car. It was too
   expensive.

8. She _____ more for the test. She would
   have done better on it.

B. Complete the conversations. Use <u>should have</u> or <u>shouldn't have</u> in the questions or responses.

1. **A:** I ate three hamburgers. I feel sick.

   B: *You shouldn't have eaten so many hamburgers.* _____.

2. **A:** Mark had coffee at 10:00 last night. He couldn't sleep.

   B: _____.

3. **A:** Natalie forgot to pay her credit card bill last month and now she has to pay a late fee.

   B: _____.

4. **A:** Hannah didn't apologize to Will and now he's upset.

   B: _____.

5. **A:** You didn't call in sick. Ms. Nguyen and I were looking for you.

   B: _____.

6. **A:** Did you really run ten miles?

   B: Yes! _____. Now my legs are sore!

7. **A:** Jerry went to bed late again last night.

   B: _____. Now, he's going to be tired all day.

8. **A:** This chicken is delicious! How's your hamburger?

   B: Terrible! _____ the chicken.

---

2. Negative <u>yes</u> / <u>no</u> questions

Negative <u>yes</u> / <u>no</u> questions

A: **Aren't** you working late tonight?
B: Yes, I am. I have a report to finish.

A: **Doesn't** he have to lose weight?
B: He really does. It's very unhealthy to be so heavy.

A: **Wasn't** he meeting us here?
B: Yes. He should be here soon.

A: **Hasn't** she done a great job on the presentation?
B: Yes, she has. It was wonderful.

Things to remember
Negative questions are used to confirm information you think is correct or to ask for agreement. Sometimes they express surprise or disbelief.

C. **Change each sentence to a negative <u>yes</u> / <u>no</u> question.**

1. They bought some juice yesterday.

   Didn't they buy some juice yesterday?

2. Ms. Cho has to watch her weight.

   _____?

3. Miss Sudan is a nice person.

   _____?

4. We agreed to meet here.

   _____?

5. You stopped eating fatty foods.

   _____?

6. Mr. Perales eats at restaurants every night.

   _____?

7. *King Kong* is a great movie.

   _____?

KING KONG
ARTS THEATER
MONDAY AND FRIDAY ONLY
Schedule of showings:
Monday 1/24: 6:00 p.m., 8:00 p.m., 10:30 p.m.
Friday 1/28: 4:45 p.m., 7:30 p.m., midnight

Monday, January 24.

D. **Complete each conversation with a negative question.**

1. **A:** <u>*Wasn't traffic bad last night?*</u>
   traffic / bad / last night

   B: I don't know. I took the train.

2. **A:** _____?
   Bob / be / here

   B: Not yet. I thought he was coming with you.

3. **A:** _____?
   Maria / like / her dress

   B: I don't think so. She's going to return it.

4. **A:** _____?
   they / need / tickets

   B: Yes, they did, but Luis had tickets for them.

5. **A:** _____?
   photocopier / make a noise

   B: Yes, it was, but it's working fine now.

UNIT 9

1. Common misspellings

A. **Complete the sentences.**

1. **A:** Where are my books?

   B: <u>*They're*</u> on the table.
   Their / They're

2. **A:** I won a million dollars.

   B: _____ kidding!
   Your / You're

3. **A:** Can you borrow from the credit union?

   B: Yes. _____ easy.
   Its / It's

4. **A:** Do they accept checks?

   B: Yes. They accept credit cards _____.
   too / two

5. **A:** Did you leave your wallet at home?

   B: Yes, and _____ I missed the bus. What a bad day!
   then / than

B. Complete the story. Choose the correct word.

	Re: weekend	

📤Send 💾Save 📇 ✒ ᴬᴮᶜ✓   📎 Insert File...   ⬆ Priority ▾   ▤Options...

ℹ   ✉

From:	Maria Santos
To:	Helen Choi
Subject:	weekend

Dear Helen,

I went _____*to*_____ visit my parents yesterday. _____
　　　　　　1. to / too　　　　　　　　　　　　　　　　　　　**2.** They're / Their

house is about _____ hours away, but _____ a nice
　　　　　　　　　3. to / two　　　　　　　　　　　　**4.** its / it's

drive. They live near my sister, Edna, who has _____ small
　　　　　　　　　　　　　　　　　　　　　　　　5. to / two

children. Edna is 10 years older _____ I am, and we get along
　　　　　　　　　　　　　　　6. than / then

well. Edna's family came _____. We all ate dinner together
　　　　　　　　　　　　　7. to / too

and _____ we went to the movies. We had a great time. Do
　　　8. than / then

you see _____ parents very often?
　　　　9. you're / your

---

2. Connecting ideas with <u>and</u>, <u>but</u>, and <u>so</u>

Two sentences can be connected with <u>and</u>, <u>but</u>, or <u>so</u>. They have different meanings.

- **Additional information:** <u>and</u>
  Mara Santala works hard, **and** she loves her job.

- **Contradictory information:** <u>but</u>
  Ms. Santala likes her job, **but** she would like better benefits.

- **Result:** <u>so</u>
  Ms. Santala's boss thinks she's a good worker, **so** he gave her a promotion.

📎 **Things to remember**
Add a comma before <u>and</u>, <u>but</u>, or <u>so</u> when connecting two sentences.

C. Combine the sentences with <u>and</u>, <u>but</u>, or <u>so</u>.

1. Ms. Flores lives in Florida. She wants to live in New York.

    Ms. Flores lives in Florida, but she wants to live in New York.

2. Tom wanted a promotion. He got more training.

    _____

3. They forgot to pay their bills. They had to pay a late fee.

    _____

4. I sleep ten hours each night. My sister sleeps only six hours a night.

    _____

5. The apartment is small. It needs to be painted.

    _____

6. The suit was very expensive. I didn't buy it.

    _____

7. Carmen didn't have any cash. She went to the ATM.

    _____

8. Tien ate at the new restaurant. He went shopping too.

    _____

9. Mark didn't have any shampoo. He didn't have any soap either.

    _____

10. Julio couldn't find the post office. He asked a woman for directions.

    _____

D. Complete the paragraph with <u>and</u>, <u>but</u>, or <u>so</u>.

Min moved to Los Angeles last month, ___and___ she started work the next day
1.

at her new job. Min likes her job very much, _____ she is making a lot of money,
2.

_____ she thinks that moving to Los Angeles was a good idea. Her husband,
3.

Sam, thinks moving was a good idea too. He got a job in Los Angeles, too,

_____ he hasn't started working yet. Sam has some free time now, _____ he
4.   5.

is going to paint the house.

Min and Sam are happy about the move, _____ their 5-year-old son, Nick, is
6.

a little upset. He was born in Korea, _____ he speaks Korean as his first
7.

language. He doesn't speak English perfectly, _____ his parents are sending
8.

him to school in the summer. Min and Sam hope that Nick learns English soon

_____ that he can make friends and enjoy life in Los Angeles.
9.

The past unreal conditional

THE PAST UNREAL CONDITIONAL

If clause (condition)					Result clause				
If	**Subject**	**had**	**Past participle**		**Subject**	**would / could**	**have**	**Past participle**	
If	I	had	arrived	yesterday	I	would	have	been	on time.
If	she	hadn't	been	sick,	she	could	have	gone	to work.
If	they	had	worked	harder,	they	would not	have	been	laid off.

Things to remember

1. You can use contractions with the past unreal conditional:

   had + not = hadn't
   would + not = wouldn't

   These contractions are only used in conversation and in informal writing:

   would + have = would've
   could + have = could've

2. As in other conditional sentences, when the <u>if</u> clause is at the beginning of the sentence, use a comma.

   If he had known about the job opening, he would have applied for the job.
   He would have applied for the job **if** he had known about the job opening.

A. **Complete the sentences. Write the letter on the line.**

1. If Mr. Rosseau hadn't finished college, ___b___

2. If I hadn't been laid off, _____

3. If Jillian and Ray hadn't taken that flight, _____

4. If you had asked me, _____

5. If Mr. McCarthy hadn't gotten a loan, _____

6. If you had been there too, _____

a. it wouldn't have been so boring.

b. he wouldn't have gotten the job.

c. I would have helped you.

d. I wouldn't have looked for a better job.

e. they would have missed the meeting.

f. he couldn't have bought the car.

B. Read the information. Check <u>True</u> or <u>False</u>.

If Jack had married his girlfriend, Maria, he would have moved to California. If he had been in California, he wouldn't have applied for the job with Clasco. If he hadn't taken the job with Clasco, he wouldn't have gone back to college for extra training. If he hadn't gone back to college, he wouldn't have taken a class in accounting. If he hadn't taken a class in accounting, he wouldn't have met Brenda. If he and Brenda hadn't met, they wouldn't have gotten married.

		True	False
1.	Jack moved to California.	❏	☑
2.	He applied for a job with Clasco.	❏	❏
3.	Jack took the job with Clasco.	❏	❏
4.	Jack didn't go back to college.	❏	❏
5.	He took a class in accounting.	❏	❏
6.	Jack married Maria.	❏	❏
7.	Jack married Brenda.	❏	❏

C. Complete each of the following past unreal conditional sentences. Use the verbs in the box.

eat	know	~~learn~~	not have	not plug	walk

1. If Mark had lived in Mexico, he <u>would have learned</u> Spanish.

2. They _____ if the bus hadn't come then.

3. We would have registered for a class if we _____ the registration date.

4. The computer wouldn't have worked if I _____ it in!

5. If you _____ the meat, you would have gotten sick.

6. If Josephine had stopped at the light, she _____ that bad accident.

D. **Read the sentences. Write a past unreal conditional sentence that has a similar meaning.**

1. I didn't get the job, so I didn't move to Chicago.

   If I had gotten the job, I would have moved to Chicago.

2. Ms. Abu felt sick, so they didn't go to the movies.

   _____

3. The weather was terrible, so they cancelled the outdoor concert.

   _____

4. Mr. Lauren didn't work hard, so he didn't get the promotion.

   _____

5. You hurt your hand, so you didn't play the piano last night.

   _____

6. I registered to vote by the deadline, so I was able to vote in the election.

   _____

7. She left her wallet at home, so she had to borrow money from a friend.

   _____

8. The laundry service didn't hire enough workers, so the customers were angry.

   _____

N O T E S

N O T E S